MISSION CRITICAL LEADERSHIP

Steve,

Great leaders never stop learning!

Semper Fidelis,
Gregg

PRAISE FOR *MISSION CRITICAL LEADERSHIP*

In Mission Critical Leadership, *Gregg Sturdevant weaves together anecdotes from his long and illustrious military career with tactical, actionable ideas that will help anyone, in any industry, become a better leader. I only wish this book had been available earlier in my career. Unlike many leadership books, this is written in an interesting, entertaining way—you may find yourself reading the entire book in one sitting.*

BELINDA NAYLOR
Vice President and Senior Marketing Strategist
Union Bank

Gregg Sturdevant's book is like food for our leadership soul! His keen insights liberate us from the thin gruel of quick-fix gimmickry pervading our society. Instead, Gregg redeems leadership as a way of life and restores it to its proper role as a master craft—worthy of our life's devotion. By focusing on the process of becoming, he stimulates your thinking and places you directly within his Marine Corps experiences so that you too can feel the mantle of leadership and the supreme satisfaction of leading, and living, well.

PAUL CALLAN
Colonel USMC (Ret.)
Creator of the Callan Course on Leadership

Gregg does a masterful job of presenting important leadership lessons he learned over the course of his thirty-seven years in uniform and applying them to corporate America. In this book, Gregg uses interesting stories from his time in the Marine Corps and industry to provide tips and tools applicable at all levels and to any size organization.

Regardless of your role, there is something to be gained by reading this book. You will come away with ideas on how to grow personally, become a stronger, more effective leader, and a better teammate. I strongly encourage you to pick up your copy today!

R. K. "SKIP" HUNTER, CLU®, JD
President
New South Investment Corporation
The First National Life Insurance Company
The American Life Assurance Corporation

Reading this book will change the way you lead yourself and others. In Mission Critical Leadership, *Gregg shares interesting and poignant stories that address issues many of us face daily while providing elegant solutions for effectively dealing with these challenges.* Mission Critical Leadership *is a great book that will inspire those who read it to become better leaders than they are today!*

SANDY LAWRENCE
Speaker, Mentor, and Military Transition Evangelist
Co-author of *The Transitioning Military* Book Series
Author of *The Transitioned Veteran: Success Beyond Service*

Seeing is believing! What better way to grow as a leader than to see a leader in action. A relatable walk of accountability, simplicity, and workforce inclusion, Gregg Sturdevant's life experiences put you inside the gears that make leaders great. His strategies of the leader/team relationship and "you" means "we" mindset will change the trajectory of organizational connections and tactical execution. Leaders that know and understand that their teams are a reflection of oneself are more apt to succeed through any circumstance. The strategies in this book will give your "we" the leadership foundation it needs by strengthening the leader in "you."

JAMI VINCENT
Founder and CEO
The WHY Solutions

General Gregg Sturdevant's Mission Critical Leadership *brings skills evolved and tested in the crucible of battle as well as everyday life. Many authors write from ivory towers who never get into the trenches, never experience the realities that exist when lives are at stake. Gregg is not one of those authors. He has lived a life where leadership failures get people killed.*

The types of leadership skills he learned on the battlefield apply equally to the corporate world. If corporations and their people are not well managed, they can fail, people can lose their jobs, their security, and their ability to support themselves and their families. It's a different type of "battle" but still very, very real.

Gregg shares his hard-knocks experience and valuable lessons learned in a book that will undoubtedly help you become a better leader. If you really want to learn leadership, if you want a text that has meat on the bone, not some airy-fairy management treatise dreamed up by someone who has never lived it, then I strongly recommend giving Mission Critical Leadership a read.

THOMAS CLAPP
Chairman of the Board
Employee Testing Center

An entertaining and informative journey from enlisted Marine to Marine General loaded with profound lessons learned over the course of a distinguished thirty-seven-year career in service to our nation. Anyone interested in the workings of Marine Corps leadership will enjoy this book. Anyone looking to be a better leader will benefit from this book. Sturdevant translates his leadership message to corporate America in a way we can all understand, relate to, and most importantly, apply in our own lives. Humility, honor, decisiveness, and compassion are key themes we need more of today. These concepts define Gregg Sturdevant—a leader you can learn from.

WALLY ADAMCHIK
President
FireStarter Speaking and Consulting
Best Selling Author of *Construction Leadership from A to Z: 26 Words to Lead By*

For a U.S. Marine, life lessons come fast and furious. For those officers who reach two stars on their chest, those lessons have been exquisitely forged into leadership principles that last a lifetime, no matter in uniform, business, or just plain life. Major General Gregg Sturdevant weaves the peaks and the valleys of an amazing military career and life story into core leadership values that will benefit anyone. Through heavy kinetics of Iraq, Afghanistan, and major battles in the halls of the Pentagon, Sturdevant gifts his readers an elegant narrative of not only what it takes to be a good leader, but how to live a leader's life.

Crisp, clean, and as sharply creased as the uniform he once wore for our Nation, Mission Critical Leadership provides readers with an invaluable and battle-tested leadership roadmap for the benefit of one's own life as well as to the success of many others.

DAVID D. SNEPP
Managing Director
CounterNarratives LLC

You cannot do any better than learning leadership tools from a battle-tested, courageous, and super-effective leader among leaders like Gregg Sturdevant. He has walked the talk! It has been said that leaders know the way, go the way, and show the way. From his lengthy and adventurous military career, retired Marine Major General Sturdevant flawlessly transforms his highly skilled leadership formulas to the private sector. You will get not only his winning philosophy but also his four tenets fortifying the key strategic and tactical paths and routes every business leader or executive will need to apply to resolve the everyday struggles and confusions of team building, crises management, and overcoming the pitfalls leaders face in getting their work done through their teams.

If you are an influencer, decision-maker, owner, or aspiring leader, this book is for you! He expresses a style of writing that is entertaining, compelling, and engaging, with stories and scenarios that are relevant to any company in any industry striving to lead the way to a better future. If you want to know how to act strategically, execute flawlessly, and lead effectively, buy this book and boost your leadership skills.

JOE YAZBECK
Founder and President
Prestige Leadership Advisors
Internationally Published Best-Selling Author
Master Speaker and Coach

MISSION CRITICAL LEADERSHIP

Marine Corps Leadership
Principles to Transform, Motivate,
and Lead Your Teams to Success

MAJOR GENERAL
GREGG STURDEVANT,
USMC (RET.)

Mission Critical Leadership
*Marine Corps Leadership Principles to Transform, Motivate,
and Lead Your Teams to Success*
Major General Gregg Sturdevant, USMC (Ret.)

Published by
Mission Critical Leadership Solutions
www.missioncriticalcoaching.net

ISBN: 978-1-7366068-0-3

**Copyright © 2021 by Mission Critical Leadership Solutions
and Gregg Sturdevant.**

All rights reserved. No part of this publication may be reproduced, distributed, or transmitted in any form or by any means, including photocopying, recording, or other electronic or mechanical methods, without the prior written permission of the publisher, except in the case of brief quotations embodied in critical reviews and certain other noncommercial uses permitted by copyright law.

For further information, please contact the author at
gregg@missioncriticalcoaching.net.

CONTENTS

Dedication xi
Foreword xiii
Introduction 1

CHAPTER 1 The Early Years 5

CHAPTER 2 Leadership is Everything! 17

CHAPTER 3 Overarching Leadership Philosophy 25

CHAPTER 4 Five Questions You Never Thought to Ask That May Be Killing Your Team! 35

CHAPTER 5 Common Sense or Lack Thereof 41

CHAPTER 6 Law of Limited Resources – How to Make the Most with the Resources at Hand 51

CHAPTER 7	Say What? You've Got to be Kidding Me!	59
CHAPTER 8	Don't Let Them Turn Their Problem into Your Problem	73
CHAPTER 9	Never Underestimate Your Instincts and Intuitions	81
CHAPTER 10	What the Hell Was That?!	93
CHAPTER 11	Leadership in Challenging Times	103
CHAPTER 12	Leaders Never Stop Learning	111
	Acknowledgement	119
	About the Author	120

DEDICATION

This book is dedicated to my family. Without their love, support, and sacrifice, I would never have been able to take advantage of the opportunities that life afforded me.

I also want to say thank you to the men and women with whom I served—you taught me so much!

FOREWORD

From dealing with toxic work environments, to fending off competition and gaining market share, to carefully using communication channels and building strategic relationships, today's demanding organizational landscape requires that leaders be exceedingly well equipped to handle the ever-increasing demands of leadership as never before.

I can honestly say that I know of no one who is more capable of teaching the leadership and organization skills necessary to thrive in this climate than General Gregg Sturdevant, USMC (Retired). This is based on having known him for over thirty-five years and interacting with him in a variety of roles, across a full spectrum of relationships including mentor, instructor, direct report, friend, colleague, and buddy (cycling, aviating, Marine).

I first met Gregg as a squadron mate in 1985. He was a First Lieutenant Marine aviator in his original tactical Squadron in the Marine Corps. I was a senior Captain in my second Squadron. From our first engagement, I realized Gregg Sturdevant was someone unique and I think you will agree as you read through this book. Interactions with him reflect a seamless merging of how he lives with how he leads – Gregg the friend, the spouse, the father, the boss, the colleague, or the subordinate each interacting with the same measure of authenticity, empathy, self-awareness, and foresight. Ask anyone who knows him, and you will hear similar comments, all reflecting admiration.

Mission Critical Leadership acquaints you with a proven leadership philosophy, honed in some of the most demanding and challenging environments you could ever imagine. Through a compendium of the author's lifetime experiences, from both the military and private organizations, you will gain direct knowledge of highly successful leadership skills and style.

With candor and wit, Gregg tells inviting stories that clearly communicate his intended messages. From these stories about real-life complex organizational problems, you will gain important insights and key leadership skills. As you read through the book you will also notice that Gregg employs a great deal of compassion and empathy, along with other elements of emotional intelligence—EI is one of the highest contributors to effective leadership, which represents a capacity for understanding how you as well as others show up in various circumstances. Further, compassion and empathy are foundational to relationship and team building. These desirable skills are demonstrated multiple times throughout the book as you will see first-hand how Gregg used these tools to effectively communicate, resolve conflict, overcome challenges, achieve a quality response from each interaction, and consistently achieve organizational goals.

In Chapter 1, you will read that Gregg believed that someone was watching out for him and that everything happens for a reason. That 'someone' was Gregg Sturdevant himself! Throughout his career, he viewed every situation from a positive perspective. Each circumstance was regarded as an opportunity. Gregg was able to assess his current state of affairs regardless of status. He then identified the necessary avenue to transform them to valuable lessons ultimately evolving challenging conditions to good and good conditions to great. Over thirty-five years, I have witnessed First Lieutenant Gregg Sturdevant seamlessly mature to Major General Gregg Sturdevant on a journey that naturally embraces the relational dimension of leadership. Now he is sharing his experience and leadership insights with anyone wanting to improve their personal and professional lives while taking their organizations to the next level.

Michael "Duffy" Dyer is a thirty plus years retired USMC Colonel, executive coach, and business executive (CEO and President of two companies) with forty plus years of extensive experience in organizational leadership, management, and leading elite teams across the globe.

BONUS FOR READERS OF MISSION CRITICAL LEADERSHIP

When the "Stuff" Hits the Fan!
Five Critical Steps for Managing a Crisis

DOWNLOAD YOUR **FREE COPY** HERE:

www.missioncriticalcoaching.net/bonus

INTRODUCTION

The lessons I learned in the military all transfer to the private sector! Certainly a bold statement, but one that I can, and will, make a case for. This book offers a compendium of timeless, simple leadership lessons. Applying these lessons can transform the way you lead, tremendously impacting your relationships and your organization.

These leadership lessons were derived from my time as a Marine. They come from a world where life or death was constantly present. Some of what I share came from combat experiences, while other leadership lessons came from military assignments in the United States.

When I took my Marine Corps uniform off and put on a civilian uniform, I quickly discovered the leadership lessons I learned while on active duty were applicable to the day-to-day operation of any company. These lessons are broad and timeless. Military stories are shared to illustrate a point, and in each case, I offer suggestions on how those leadership lessons apply to corporate America.

It is certainly bold to say that all the leadership lessons I learned in the military transfer to the private sector. But I assure you that when individuals and organizations adhere to the leadership lessons I share, they do well. When they are ignored, businesses fail.

Before starting this book, I spent a fair amount of time categorizing the leadership lessons I learned over nearly thirty-seven years of wearing a Marine Corps uniform. I then went through and selected the stories that I thought most relevant to the corporate world. What you will find are examples of events I experienced or problems I had to address while on active duty. I provide interesting vignettes and map them to the experiences I had in the private sector.

If you were to Google "Why people quit their jobs," you would find "terrible bosses" in the top three nearly every time. An associate recently shared that 85 percent of people interviewed (unfortunately, she did not provide the source) left their jobs because of a bad boss. *Bulanetwork.com* reports that 75 percent of workers who voluntarily left their jobs did so because of their bosses and not the position itself.[1] There is no excuse for not being the best leader you can be—your employees deserve the absolute best. This book offers insight that, if believed and embraced, will help you grow personally and professionally.

Over the course of my career, I witnessed more than my share of examples of failed leadership. Along the way, I closely observed my leaders, took detailed notes, and spent countless hours thinking about how I would do business if I ever had the opportunity to lead a group of Marines.

I was honored and privileged to lead Marines and sailors in four different command tours. As a Captain, I was fortunate to be selected as a Detachment Officer in charge of fourteen Marines for a six-month pre-deployment workup followed by a six-month

---

[1] Grow Great with Randy Cantrell. *"YOU Are The Reason People Are Quitting Their Jobs #4021."* (bulanetwork.com)

INTRODUCTION

deployment to the Mediterranean. Nine years later, I scaled up to squadron command as a Lieutenant Colonel. I lead 525 Marines and Sailors and an equal number of family members spread across two locations in southern California and an additional site in Yuma, Arizona. That was an amazing time for me. I had an incredible team and was privileged to lead Marines in combat in Afghanistan (2002). My command tour was extended, and I took the squadron into Iraq (2003) for the beginning of Operation Iraqi Freedom.

Later as a Colonel, I commanded a unit comprised of 2,300 personnel; some of the finest men and women to serve in the Marine Corps and Navy. This assignment included another pre-deployment workup followed by a seven-month deployment to the Middle East.

My final command tour found me back in Afghanistan, the land of not-quite-right. In February 2012, I took the Third Marine Aircraft Wing (Forward) into Helmand Province, Afghanistan. There, I commanded twelve U.S. squadrons, totaling 3,500 US personnel plus 1,000 British soldiers and well over 125 aircraft.

Each command tour involved accepting increased responsibility. I successfully applied my leadership philosophy to each of those assignments. Along the way, I captured many lessons that are shared throughout this book.

As I approached squadron command as a Lieutenant Colonel, I developed a leadership philosophy applicable to nearly every situation a leader could face. This philosophy, described in detail in these pages, applies at the individual, team, and overall organizational level. It can even be applied to your personal life.

Unlike many of the states, the military is not an at-will employment organization. Service members sign a contract with the government of the United States of America. Signing that contract comes with expectations. Beginning with the expectation that you will complete your enlistment. You will train. You will be a team player. You will do your absolute best. There are many more "*you wills*," but you get the picture.

The military is a truly diverse group, with people coming from a variety of backgrounds. The challenge is to motivate these people to rise to the occasion and be the best they can be. Sometimes things go well and other times not so much.

People mistakenly believe that men and women in the military will automatically follow orders. This is true in most, but not all, cases. The follow-up question is whether they are doing their best when they follow orders. The challenge is to get them to do their absolute best. How do you inspire them to perform up to their potential? That is where emotional intelligence (EI) comes into play. The really good leaders recognize the importance of incorporating EI into their leadership style. By doing so, they can take an organization that would normally perform at the average level and pull them up to the above average, and occasionally, the great level.

This book provides tools and tips that will challenge your self-awareness and make you a better leader. By applying my leadership philosophy, you will grow both personally and professionally. Equally important, your teams will perform better.

I invite you to join me for an adventure that lasted nearly four decades.

★ CHAPTER ONE ★

THE EARLY YEARS

"You just can't beat the person who never gives up."

– BABE RUTH, LEGENDARY BASEBALL PLAYER

With my father's encouragement, I began collecting leadership lessons long before I joined the Marine Corps and continued that practice once I enlisted. Over a forty-year period, I wore a Marine uniform for nearly thirty-seven years and had the pleasure of serving under some of the finest leaders our country has ever produced, as well as a few weak ones, always observing and always taking notes.

I am writing this book to pass on some of the more important leadership lessons I learned from being in the military and, later, working in corporate America. Lessons that I think you will find interesting and applicable to your personal and professional life.

Let me begin by telling you about my family, give you an understanding of how I was raised, and share some of the career highlights that got me to where I am today. Telling you my story will give you tools and tips that you can apply to lead yourself or lead others.

Looking back, I do not think there was ever a doubt that I would grow up to be anything other than a Marine.

Oldest of three kids—two boys and a girl, I was raised in a two-parent family in the Midwest. My dad was an active-duty Marine for the first eight years of his military career. However, by the time three kids came along, my mother was really not interested in my dad staying on active duty and moving our young family every few years. So, he transferred into the Reserve Infantry Battalion in Kansas City, Missouri, and became a toy salesman for a large toy manufacturer. My mother was originally a stay-at-home mom but would eventually have to work to support our family after my father's health failed.

THE EARLY YEARS

In January of 1964 we moved from Kansas City to St. Louis. My parents were building a house on the outskirts of St. Louis County, so we moved into a duplex for six-months waiting for it to be finished. We would soon be the fifth family to move into a subdivision that would eventually have a couple of thousand homes.

Living in a construction zone for a few years while the neighborhood was being built out was a blast. The area surrounding our new neighborhood was all farmland. Two young boys could not have asked for a better playground. Dirt everywhere. A great place to play *Cowboys and Indians* or *War*.

Later, when we were old enough to have BB guns, we would ride our bikes out to the remaining open pastures and have BB gunfights. On several occasions, I came close to shooting my brother's eye out . . . how dumb were we?

When I was about halfway through high school, my father got sick and was unable to continue working. My mother, who had been a stay-at-home wife my entire life, went back to school to learn a skill so she could provide for the family. Roles were reversed. My mother worked, and my father maintained the house.

To pull my share of the load, I quit sports my senior year of high school and entered a school/work program where I went to school in the morning and worked in the afternoon. This worked well for me; it allowed me to make money so I could go on dates. However, I did not focus on my studies, and I would pay for that shortsightedness multiple times in the future.

As high school graduation approached in the spring of 1975, I needed to figure out what was coming next, and I knew it was not going to be college. I was a C student and had no interest in sticking around St. Louis so I could attend one of the local community colleges. It was time for me to make my own way. I needed to grow up, a lot, and take some pressure off my parents. My leaving meant there would be one less mouth to feed.

IT'S A GREAT WAY OF LIFE!

The Vietnam War was wrapping up, and the Air Force was running a commercial, "It's a great way of life!" I convinced myself that I was going to enlist in the Air Force. I was not focusing on the Air Force to torture my Marine father; I just thought their advertisement was attractive. So, one day, I drove to an L-shaped strip mall with recruiting offices for each of the services. I parked at the far end of the parking lot in the only available space. To get to the Air Force Recruiting office, I would have to walk past the Navy, Marine Corps, and Army recruiting offices.

As I was walking down the sidewalk, I passed the Navy office. It was dark inside, with no sign of human life. When I got to the Marine Corps recruiting office, a Sergeant was standing in the doorway looking sharp in dress blue trousers and a khaki shirt. He asked me where I was going. I pointed to the right and told him I was on my way to join the Air Force. He literally grabbed me by the collar and said, "You don't want to join the Air Force. You want to be a Marine!" How could he tell?

Needless to say, I never made it to the Air Force recruiting office.

When I went home and told my parents that I would be joining the Marine Corps, I think my father went into his bedroom and closed the door and gave a silent yell.

Now that I had decided to be a Marine, I still was not fully committed. A carryover from the tail end of the Vietnam War was a two-year enlistment option. You had to be in boot camp by the last day of June 1975 to qualify. For whatever reason, I did not go down to the enlistment center until after I graduated high school in early June. As I was progressing through the physical, I found myself being examined by a bunch of old doctors. It turned out I have flat feet and would have to seek a waiver. By the time my waiver came back, June thirtieth had come and gone.

When I returned to MEPS (Military Enlistment Processing Station) to complete my physical and the enlistment paperwork, I was working with a lady who was using a typewriter to complete my enlistment contract. When she got to the "length of service" block on the form, she asked me how long I was enlisting for. I proudly told her, "Three years." She replied, "If we had known you were only enlisting for three years, we never would have sent your waiver." I am not sure there was any truth to that statement but it did make me rethink the length of my contract. With that, I decided to enlist for four years. I took my first-ever airplane flight later that day to Lindbergh Field, San Diego, to attend boot camp at the Marine Corps Recruit Depot.

While I was in boot camp, I received word that I was to report to the Series Commander (a Captain and the person in charge of the 320 recruits assigned to the company). I went through the long and painful procedures required to gain entry into the Captain's office. After I finished reporting, he asked me one simple question. He wanted to know how my grades were in high school. I sounded off in a loud, proud voice that "the private was a C student." I received a one-word response, "Dismissed!" Back to training I went. I had the GCT (General Classification Test) score to be an officer but not the high school grades to go to the Naval Academy Preparatory School, which was the reason for the question.

HEY LIEUTENANT, I WANT YOUR JOB

Two years later, I applied for the Marine Enlisted Commissioning Education Program (MECEP). MECEP was used to identify enlisted Marines that were qualified for consideration for commissioning. Enlisted Marines selected for MECEP went to a college or university of their choice, remained on active duty, and received their pay and a small stipend to help defer the costs of attending school. There were 450 enlisted Marines applying for 150 slots. Although I had recently been meritoriously promoted to Corporal, I was not selected. It is hard to be competitive with C grades, so I started going to college at night to prove that I was college material.

The following year, I was in Okinawa, Japan with the Third Marine Division when I attempted to apply for the Broaden Opportunity for Officer Selection Training (BOOST), which was essentially the same process as MECEP. BOOST was designed to send selectees to a prep school to prepare them to attend The Naval Academy in Annapolis, Maryland.

You need to understand the amount of work required to put together a MECEP or BOOST package. You must take a physical fitness test (PFT), receive a comprehensive physical, gather all your transcripts, write a paper on why you wanted to be an officer, have an official photo taken, and appear before a three-officer panel where you are asked questions on why you want to be an officer.

Two weeks after the BOOST board met back in Washington, DC, the Third Marine Division Career Planner in Okinawa walked up to me to give me my package back. He explained to me he didn't have time to endorse it—maybe next year. There was not going to be a next year. My enlistment was going to be up the following summer, and I was going to get out so I could go back to college. I knew if I did not at least try college as a full-time student, I would always regret it; even if I failed, I would have at least given it an honest shot.

After I was honorably discharged in 1979, I returned to St. Louis and moved in with my parents while I worked two part-time jobs and used the GI Bill to attend a couple of local community colleges. The same community colleges that I swore I would never go to. After a year and a half, I was on my way to Southeast Missouri State University in Cape Girardeau, Missouri. I was working on

a bachelor's degree in business administration with a minor in political science and really was not sure what I wanted to do after graduation.

SO, YOU WANT TO BE A MARINE (AGAIN)?

In the spring of my Junior year, shortly after arriving in Cape Girardeau, I found out the Marine Reserve unit from St. Louis was going to Norway for their two-week annual training cycle. I had never been to Norway, so I thought I would give it a shot. I wandered down to the local Marine Recruiter's office in Cape Girardeau. When I walked in, I met Gunnery Sergeant Jesse Todd.

I told him I wanted to join the Reserves. He explained to me that I did not want to go into the Reserves . . . I needed to go on active duty. I gave Gunnery Sergeant Todd a quick rundown on my background. The next thing I knew, he was on the phone with the Officer Selection Officer in St. Louis. He asked me if I could be in downtown St. Louis on Saturday morning at 9:30 am. I said I would be there. Gunnery Sergeant Todd got me started on the road to becoming an officer. He could have easily signed me up for the reserves, but instead, he did the right thing and turned me over to the Officer Selection Officer.

I still speak to "retired" Master Sergeant Todd at least once a year. He is enjoying a second retirement outside Branson, Missouri.

That Spring (1981), I worked with the Officer Selection Officer and scrambled to put together an application for Officer Candidate School. I finally received word on a Friday in early June that I had been accepted for the Platoon Leader Class (Combined) Program and shipped to Quantico, Virginia, the following Monday.

During the Fall of 1981, I took the AQT/FAR (Aviation Qualification Test / Flight Aptitude Rating) and scored well enough to qualify for an Aviation Contract. I took the flight physical and was set to sign the aviation guarantee prior to Christmas, but I never did. I was struggling with whether I wanted to fly machines or lead Marines. It wasn't until later in my career that I realized being a pilot allowed me to fly and lead at the same time.

I reported to The Basic School in Quantico, Virginia (approximately thirty miles south of Washington, DC) in August 1982 on an open contract, meaning I could be assigned to any Military Occupational Specialty (MOS) in the Marine Corps. The Basic School is the first stop for all newly commissioned Marine officers. You spend six months getting a general education on how the various parts of the Marine Corps work and a specific education on infantry tactics to ensure every Marine officer is capable of leading

THE EARLY YEARS

Marines in combat. It did not take me long to come to the realization that I wanted to give flying a try. By the time our final field exercise rolled around, I was convinced that I had made a good decision by selecting aviation.

I finished flight school in a year and then went to California to transition into the helicopter that I would fly in the fleet. From there, I was off to Hawaii for my first fleet tour in CH-46 helicopters. I spent four years in Hawaii. Over half my time there was spent off-island, either deployed to Okinawa, Japan, or off at a school somewhere on the mainland. No complaints—by the time my four years were up, I had 2,200 hours of flight time and was an advanced tactics instructor.

From Hawaii, I found myself back in Pensacola as a flight instructor. I was on my second deployment to Okinawa when my orders first came in. I briefly looked at them and saw Pensacola, so I figured I was good to go. About two weeks later, the squadron Administration Officer came running down the hall to inform me that my orders were indeed to Pensacola but not to Whiting Field,

where the student pilots began the flying phase of training. I was being assigned to main side Pensacola to be a full-time academic instructor and a part-time flight instructor. I halfheartedly fought the orders. I was not comfortable with public speaking, I figured speaking in front of people every day would help me improve my communication skills.

THE BEST THING THAT EVER HAPPENED TO ME

Shortly after I arrived in Pensacola, my Commanding Officer, a Navy Captain (a senior officer, one rank below Rear Admiral; equal to Colonel in the other services), called a Navy Lieutenant and me into his office and told us he wanted us to represent him at an American Cancer Society fundraiser. Apparently, several members of the Pensacola Snow Skiing Club, to which he belonged, were also members of the American Cancer Society. I was not even aware that Pensacola had a snow skiing club.

I will not go into all the details, but I will tell you that it was one of the best nights of my life—I met my future wife that night. I was running late for a funding raising event and almost ran her over as she stepped out in front of my pickup truck. She literally had to jump out of the way to keep from getting hit. I got a quick look at this pretty little redhead as I drove by. I immediately parked my truck and went inside to find her so I could apologize. That is when I met Tina and her friend, Alicia. A year and a half later, we were married, and the rest is history.

Some years later (In 1999), I was being looked at for command. I figured with my background, I would be as competitive as anyone else out there. I ended up being on the alternate list that year, meaning if someone could not take command for whatever reason, then the Marine Corps would turn to the alternate list to find a suitable replacement. Boy was I pissed. The next year, after moving the family from northern Virginia down to Jacksonville, North Carolina, I was slated for an operational squadron on the West Coast and ended up getting extended in command and deployed the squadron to combat twice. I am convinced that this west coast command tour led to my selection for Colonel command and later to Brigadier General.

Two combat tours in a single squadron command tour was highly unusual, combining that with my extensive shipboard experience and my combat performance evaluations led to a promotion to Colonel and selection to command a Marine Expeditionary Unit (MEU).

MEU command went well but did not last a full three years. I had already completed one workup and deployment cycle to the Middle East and was deep into a second workup when I received word I had been selected for promotion to Brigadier General and assignment to be the Director, Public Affairs, United States Marine Corps.

SOMEONE WAS WATCHING OUT FOR ME

I firmly believe that everything happens for a reason. If I had enlisted for two years, I would have reenlisted and never looked back. If I had been selected for MECEP or BOOST or received orders to

Whiting Field instead of main side Pensacola, my timing would have been off. I would have never met Tina, and I wouldn't be where I am today—happily married and living in Tampa, Florida.

It really should not come as a surprise that I ended up enlisting in the Marine Corps. I had been around Marines my whole life. Some of those old guys have known me since I was a little boy. They set a great example for me, showed me what being a man looked like, they had strong work ethics and solid moral compasses.

Now that you have a better understanding of where I came from and who I am, we can shift over to the subject at hand. The remainder of the book is dedicated to sharing lessons I learned throughout my Marine Corps career and my time in the private sector.

★ CHAPTER TWO ★

LEADERSHIP IS EVERYTHING!

"The secret to success is good leadership, and good leadership is all about making the lives of your team members or workers better."

– QUOTEREEL.COM

As I discussed in the introductory chapter, I enlisted in the Marine Corps for a couple of reasons. In simplest terms, I needed to get out on my own and grow up, and it took some pressure off my family. I did not realize it at the time, but my graduate-level education in leadership was about to begin in boot camp.

AT THE MOST BASIC LEVEL, YOU MUST LEARN TO LEAD YOURSELF BEFORE YOU CAN LEAD OTHERS

During the summer of 1975, the Vietnam War was winding down, and it was a tough time to be in uniform. The draft had just ended, and the country was struggling to heal after a very unpopular and protracted war. The military had huge issues, drug and alcohol abuse, race relations issues, and poor leadership.

Boot camp was unlike anything I had ever experienced, which I am sure was, and still is, the same for most recruits. The Marine Corps has twelve weeks to break you down and rebuild you into the person they want you to be. This is one of the characteristics that makes Marines different from the other services. The Marine Corps is not looking for a bunch of unique individuals. They take men and women from every walk of life and mold them into physically fit and confident people who know how to defend themselves and our country.

In boot camp, we spent countless hours on the parade deck marching. Why marching? It teaches you to respond instantly to orders. Think back to World War II. Can you imagine a team leader

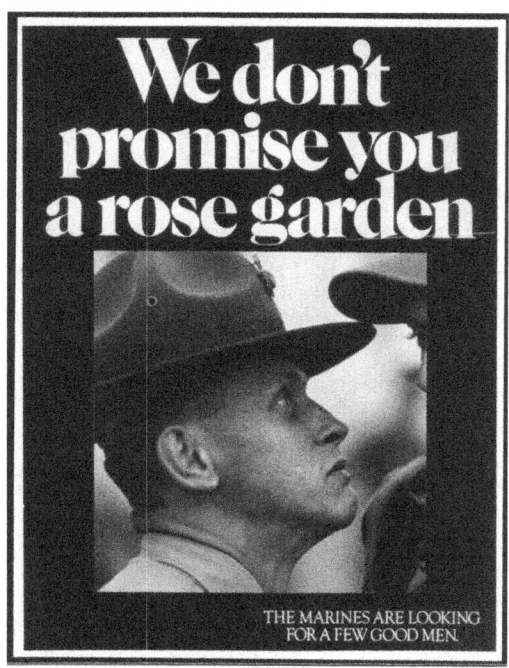

giving the command, "Take the hill!" and instead of charging forward, they stopped to think about what might happen?

What the Marine Corps was doing was teaching us to lead ourselves. You must know how to lead yourself before you can lead others. The same goes for officers.

ALL OFFICERS ARE NOT CREATED EQUAL

Do not get me wrong, the Marine Corps had some amazing leaders, but that has not always been the case. As we know, all leaders are not created equal. Many of the officers I served under while I was enlisted were the product of Reserve Officer Training Corps (ROTC) programs. The quality spread was broad. Much of their professionalism depended on the quality of the active-duty officer instructors at their college or university.

I once worked around a First Lieutenant who did not know how to properly wear his uniform, which was a bit of a surprise since he had graduated from a southern military college. Even though I was just a junior enlisted man, I would routinely have to remind him to square his uniform away. On one occasion, he told me, "I had to do that when I was in school. I don't have to do that anymore." He clearly did not understand what the Marine Corps expected from those who wear the uniform or his role as a leader.

The Naval Academy was not much better. Every year, roughly 20-22 percent of graduating midshipmen are commissioned in the Marine Corps. They also followed the model I just described—some were superb officers, others were far from it.

I am sure the same goes for the corporate sector. All leaders are not created equal.

As John C. Maxwell so famously quoted, "People don't care how much you know until they know how much you care."

Simon Sinek's book, *Leaders Eat Last*, masterfully captures this sentiment. This is about putting your employees first. For many leaders, this is a foreign concept, literally.

> "People don't care how much you know until they know how much you care."

Let me give you an example. In 2007, my military unit was in Kenya working with the African Rifles, a Kenyan infantry battalion. The commander of the U.S. Marine Corps infantry battalion came to me with a request to host a "Warrior Night" dinner for our Kenyan counterparts. I thought it was a great idea and an excellent opportunity to strengthen our relationship with the Kenyans. A plan was developed, contracts were let, and food and drink were trucked up from Mombasa, which turned out to be quite a logistical challenge.

On the night of the dinner, we pulled everyone out of the field in time to participate in the festivities. The evening started with a social hour. For the senior officers, that meant sitting in a circle getting to know each other better. When dinner was announced, the Kenyan officers immediately stood and headed to the chow line. We stopped them and explained that we always let the troops eat first. Why? We want to ensure our men and women get enough to eat. If there's anything left over, then the officers get to eat. We all sat back down, had another beer, and waited for our turn to eat.

This was not an isolated incident. During that deployment, we conducted military exercises in several Middle East countries. Each exercise followed a building block approach to training. We started with individual training and then worked our way up to unit tactics. The grand finale was the FINEX (final exercise). Each FINEX was attended by the country's senior military leaders and a few politicians. Elaborate viewing stands were temporarily constructed, and massive amounts of food and drink were present. As a guest, I always took my lead from the host. In some countries,

> "Success or failure of an organization is dependent on leadership—it's that simple!"

the leaders ate heartily while observing the big attack. In other countries, they ate very little. Regardless, as soon as the exercise concluded and the senior leaders stepped away from the viewing area, the place was swarmed by the conscript soldiers fighting over the leftover food.

SUCCESS OR FAILURE OF AN ORGANIZATION IS DEPENDENT ON LEADERSHIP—IT'S THAT SIMPLE!

So how does an organization ensure they have strong leaders in place? First, they recognize that leaders are present at all levels, not just at the top of the organization. Second, they look to the future and focus on recruiting, hiring, and retaining top talent. Third, they invest in training and accept the fact they might lose people they really do not want to lose.

LEADERS ARE PRESENT AT ALL LEVELS

Leaders are present at all levels. How does this happen? Sometimes, it's by accident. Ideally, the company identifies employees they see as having potential and coaches and mentors them. These individuals then grow personally and professionally and, hopefully, stay with the organization.

When recruiting, hiring, and retaining top talent, what is your organization's reputation? Do you pay a fair market wage? Do you have a high turnover? Is this because you are viewed as a good place to start but don't really offer long-term opportunities to grow?

Avoid hiring toxic people; some companies conduct personality assessments and intelligence tests as part of the screening process. If someone with an antisocial personality slips into the organization, get rid of them. It continues to amaze me that companies hold on to these people. Why? Because they are competent? I worked for a company that had someone who fell into that category. That person was competent but divisive, contributed nothing to the sales team, and negatively influenced a direct report to the point that the direct report acted similarly. That individual was eventually released long after it should have happened. The divisive employee should have been terminated, and the direct report put on a ninety-day performance improvement plan to see if the bad behavior could be corrected.

INVEST IN YOUR EMPLOYEE'S FUTURE

Train all—coach and mentor the most promising. I know I am repeating myself, but I have more to say on this subject. Gone are the days where you hire someone, and they work for you for thirty or forty years before retiring. You need to recognize that some of the people you invest time and effort into may choose to move on for a variety of reasons. That is the world we live in today. They move on, and you replace them with someone who is as good, or better, than the person who just left.

> "Train all—coach and mentor the most promising."

The probability of holding onto a top performer improves when you are able to map out their career paths. For example, engineers fall into that category. Engineers begin their careers as an Engineer 1. Over time and with proven performance, they move up the scale from Engineer 1 to Engineer 2, then Engineer 3, and finally

Engineer 4. The sales side, where I worked, was not as clean. For sales representatives, there must be a career progression plan identified that blends both promotions and a compensation package, with more weight being placed on the latter.

WHEN THE GOING GETS TOUGH, TRUE LEADERS SHINE

It is much easier to lead when things are going well. The real test comes when challenges arise. Strong leaders rise to the occasion when things get rough. They do not play the "woe is me" card. Instead, they see opportunities where others see obstacles. Strong leaders offer/identify solutions to hard problems.

CHAPTER TAKEAWAYS:

1. At the most basic level, you must learn to lead yourself before you can lead others.
2. Success or failure of an organization is dependent on leadership.
3. Leaders are present at all levels.
4. Invest in your employee's future, recognizing that they may or may not stay with your organization.

Leveraging the leadership lessons I learned in the Marine Corps, I developed a leadership philosophy that works at all levels, across all industries. You will learn more about that philosophy and the tenets it encompasses in the following chapters.

★ CHAPTER THREE ★

OVERARCHING LEADERSHIP PHILOSOPHY

"Become the leader you would want to follow."
– GERARD ADAMS

Have you ever found yourself asking, "How in the world did this person get into this key leadership position? They are incapable of leading themselves, much less someone else!" I have, numerous times, both in and out of uniform.

LEADERS COME IN ALL SHAPES AND SIZES

Over the course of my nearly thirty-seven-years in uniform, I was exposed to a variety of leadership styles. Some were really good, and others were far from it. And as one of my "not-so-good" commanders once said, "You learn as much from the bad leaders as you do from the good." Wise words.

When I was selected to command a helicopter squadron as a Lieutenant Colonel, I knew I had to come up with my commander's guidance to share with the men and women I would be entrusted to lead and keep safe. It was a matter of making time to form a leadership philosophy.

At the time, I was knee-deep in budget battles in the Pentagon and really did not have a chance to think about what was coming next. I was excited for the opportunity to be heading to command, but I really needed to focus on the task at hand. The Marine Corps was kind enough to help me find time to think about my future responsibilities.

Twice a year, the Marine Corps runs a two-week "commander's course" at Quantico, Virginia. This course is intended to prepare commanders and their spouses for command. Over the two weeks, you learn about the art of command, family readiness programs, receive media training, etc. Some of the sessions are joint (commander and spouse), while others are separated based on each topic for the appropriate audience.

WHAT'S YOUR LEADERSHIP PHILOSOPHY?

When I finally got to Quantico, I had time to slow down and think about how I would lead the squadron. I thought about my previous commanders and the life experiences I had and came up with four things I thought essential to being a good leader. They are set people

> **GREGG'S LEADERSHIP PHILOSOPHY**
>
> 1. Set your team up for success
> 2. Use common sense in decision making
> 3. Look for ways to "work smarter, not harder"
> 4. Ensure effective communication

up for success, use common sense, work smarter, not harder, and communicate effectively.

YOUR SUCCESS DEPENDS ON THEIR SUCCESS

Set your team up for success; I saw this as my primary responsibility as a commander. I needed to ensure my entire workforce had the tools and training needed to do their jobs. This concept cascades. My job as a leader was to set my direct reports up for success. If they had direct reports, then our job (my job combined with my direct reports) was to set their direct reports up for success. Just continue with that line of thought. For example:

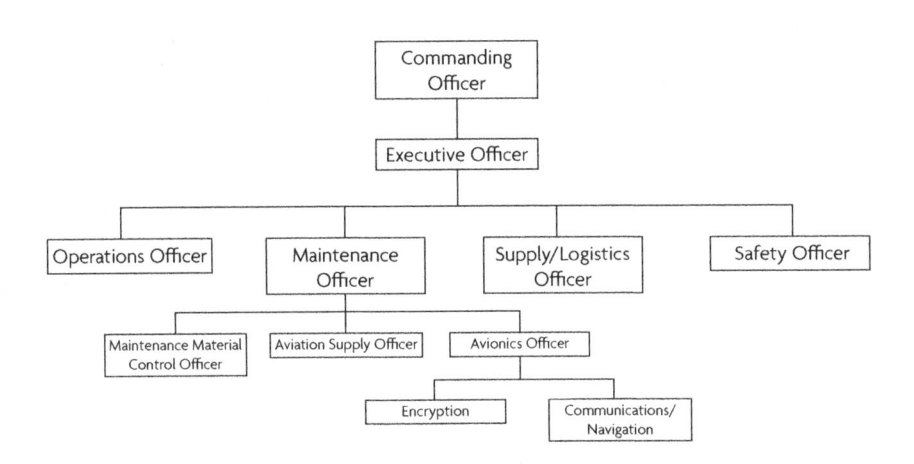

```
                        Commanding
                         Officer
                            |
                     Executive Officer
    _____|_____
    |              |                |              |
Operations    Maintenance      Supply/Logistics   Safety Officer
 Officer        Officer            Officer
               ____|____
               |       |
        Maintenance  Aviation    Avionics Officer
        Material     Supply         ____|____
        Control      Officer        |       |
        Officer                 Encryption  Communications/
                                            Navigation
```

In the notional organization chart above, the commanding officer is responsible for setting the executive officer up for success. Together, they are responsible for setting the operations officer, maintenance officer, supply/logistics officer, and safety officer up for success. In turn, the commanding officer, executive officer, and maintenance officer are responsible for the success of the maintenance material control officer, the aviation supply officer, and the avionics officer. Finally, the commanding officer, executive officer, maintenance officer, and avionics officer are responsible for setting up the encryption section and communication/navigation shop for success. This is simply a waterfall effect.

When one of your direct reports stumbles, the first question that needs answering is, "What could I have done better to set this person up for success?" Are they in the right position, or would they perform better in a different role? What skills does this person bring to the organization, and where would they be best suited? What training is needed for them to be effective at their job? Did they receive the necessary training to do their job? How are outside influences impacting their performance? The list could go on and on.

> "What could I have done better to set this person up for success?"

There were several times where I moved someone from one department to another because of substandard performance. I knew my people well enough to know when someone was not happy in their current position. I would bring them in and sit them down in my office, and we would have a heart-to-heart talk. I wanted to hear how they thought things were going, and I needed to know if they were happy where they were. Those talks usually resulted in that person being reassigned to a role that I thought they were better suited for. I always circled back after about a month to see how they liked their new job.

Along those same lines, I emphasized the importance of continual job performance feedback. The Marine Corps had a program where you were directed to sit down with the Marines you were responsible for and provide counseling every six months. The objective was to provide an honest assessment, both good and bad, and document the discussion. If there was a performance issue, then the counseling session needed to include documented performance improvement steps. Expectations and the time allotted for improvement needed to be spelled out so that there were no misunderstandings.

Think about how you can apply this concept to your direct reports.

COMMON SENSE—IF ONLY IT WERE MORE COMMON

My second point is tied to common sense. I am originally from St. Louis, Missouri (the "Show-Me" state) and was raised by parents that used common sense to go through life. I follow that same line of thinking. I always told my people that a simple plan, well-executed, would carry the day. And if they needed to make a decision when I wasn't around to default to common sense.

THERE'S GOT TO BE A BETTER WAY OF DOING BUSINESS

The third point is to work smarter, not harder. This leadership nugget came about because I grew tired of hearing senior Marines, both enlisted and officer, tell me, "This is how we've always done it." You want to watch my head explode, use those words.

No company or military unit has the luxury of excess bodies. Manpower and material shortfalls are a daily challenge that must be overcome. We must get creative with our problem solving, and find ways to work smarter, not harder.

Often times, as someone moves up the ladder, they become less engrossed in day-to-day activities in a specific area and take on a role that has them overseeing multiple activities. That was certainly true in the military. In the senior ranks, we used to say our knowledge base was, "A mile wide and an inch deep." We knew a little about a lot of things, but if we had to drill down, we would probably need to reach out to someone else to help answer the questions.

I used to remind people that we really needed to ensure that every voice was heard. It is the people doing the heavy lifting who would often come up with ideas of how to do things better, more efficiently, at a lower cost, etc. They are the ones driving process improvement. Even in the military, no one should be afraid to share an opinion or idea. We used to joke, "It took a college education to fly the aircraft and a high school education to fix the aircraft."

THERE IS NO SUBSTITUTE FOR EFFECTIVE COMMUNICATION

Later, after I had been extended in squadron command and was preparing for a second shipboard combat deployment, this time to Iraq, I added another point . . . communication. Effective communication, to be exact. Message sent, message received, message understood, and message acted upon.

The previous deployment had been painful. The ship's commander did not understand the Marines' chain of command. Any time he had an issue with my squadron, he came looking for me. He was often upset because we needed to fly when he did not want to open the flight deck. He could not comprehend that I had received tasking from my higher headquarters, and if he did not like it, he could go see my boss. He never complained to my boss. Instead, he continued to literally put his finger in my chest.

That same commander refused to trust his people. Every, and I mean even the smallest, most inconsequential decision, had to go all the way to the ship's commanding officer. What a waste of time—what a negative impact that had on his people—he was telling them he did not trust them. When he took command, he inherited a talented team. By the time his two-year command tour was up, he had run every (no exaggeration) junior officer out of the Navy. A portion of the Navy's future voted with their feet by walking out the door. How sad!

EFFECTIVE COMMUNICATION IS A MUST FOR SUCCESSFUL LEADERS

My main takeaway from the year that I was associated with that Navy Captain was the importance of effective communication. We returned from that deployment, and approximately fifty percent of the officers in the squadron and all the Majors (mid-level leaders with 10-16 years of experience) left for their next assignments. I got a new batch of copilots and four new Majors, and we began to rebuild the squadron. Normally squadrons had eighteen months between deployments, but the attack on 9/11 changed things. Not only did it cause us to leave for the deployment mentioned above six weeks early. We also ended up deploying on short notice a second time, exactly seven months to the day from when we had returned home from our last deployment. I got extended in command and was not about to complain.

The first thing I did when I found out that I had just eight days to prepare the squadron for combat *and* get them reembarked aboard the ship was to take four of my key officers with me to visit the ship that would carry us to combat. When we met with our Navy counterparts aboard the ship, I explained what I had experienced on the previous deployment, told them that I would accept 50 percent of the blame, and made it clear that it wasn't going to happen again. I explained that I expected all parties to work the problem out at the lowest possible level.

Effective communication and cooperation would be required to get through the coming months. Setting expectations early worked magnificently. Everyone had a completely different attitude on this deployment, including the ship's commanding officer, who did his best to ensure the Marines had everything we needed when we left the ship six-weeks later and flew into Iraq.

EMPOWER YOUR WORKFORCE, AND YOU WILL EARN THEIR TRUST

The other benefit that arose from this effective communication discussion was the sense of empowerment my officers felt. They knew I trusted their judgment and had their backs. This paid big dividends during the run into Baghdad. One of our primary missions was to provide CASEVAC (casualty evacuation) for then Major General

James Mattis and the First Marine Division. This meant sending a section (a section equals two) of aircraft to shadow assigned infantry units. The section leader would call me on an iridium satellite phone once a day to check-in and report this section's flight status. Sections would normally be gone for at least two days at a time. That was a lot of responsibility for a Captain to shoulder, but they performed superbly. They did everything that was asked of them and more. In fact, thanks to the team's performance, our squadron won the 2003 Marine Corps Aviation Association's Edward C. Dyer Award for being the best Marine medium helicopter squadron in the Marine Corps!

We will take a deeper look at each of these four leadership tenets in subsequent chapters.

CHAPTER TAKEAWAYS:

1. Applying these four leadership tenets leads to success. Without them, your team will likely not align with your vision, and there is a good chance your company will become stagnant and could potentially fail.
2. Your success depends on their success.
3. Use common sense in decision making and planning.
4. Challenge your team to find better ways to do business.
5. Effective communication is a must for successful leaders.
6. Empower your workforce, and you will earn their trust.

★ CHAPTER FOUR ★

FIVE QUESTIONS YOU NEVER THOUGHT TO ASK THAT MAY BE KILLING YOUR TEAM!

"Earn your success based on service to others, not at the expense of others."

– H. JACKSON BROWN, JR.

You should have seen the look on "The Knife's" face when I told him that if the squadron was ordered to war, I was not going!

"What? Why?" Sife the Knife demanded.

I swallowed hard and told him, "I'm not going to war because our squadron is not combat-ready!"

"Sife the Knife" was the nickname of our new squadron executive officer (second in command). At the time, I had been in the squadron for a year, but I hadn't yet started my tactical flight training. I was months behind my peers in sister squadrons. The sad part about it was that every other copilot in my squadron was also behind. How "Sife the Knife" reacted to my outburst reveals much of what someone should do to be a successful leader.

In my nearly thirty-seven years in uniform, I've been exposed to numerous leadership styles, some superb and inspiring, others far from it. Once again, as one of my commanders once said, "You learn as much from the bad leaders as you do from the good."

What I've learned is this: Setting your team up for success is the primary responsibility of a superb leader. I would love to tell you every leader I've served with has had this same philosophy, but it would be a lie. There are good leaders and bad, both in the military and in the business world.

> "Setting your team up for success is the primary responsibility of a superb leader."

FIVE QUESTIONS YOU NEVER THOUGHT TO ASK

JOB FEEDBACK IS ESSENTIAL

In one instance during one of the six-month performance reviews mentioned earlier, the head of my administrative section was struggling with her job. We had one of those heart-to-heart discussions and ended up making a deal: If she gave me everything she had, then I would take care of her. I was not responsible for writing her annual performance assessment, but I was the one to review the report. Her direct supervisor wrote the annual report, and it was not pretty. After she received the review, we sat down for another talk. She had, in fact, given 110 percent of what she was able to provide—but she still fell short of where her peers were.

Next, I talked to her supervisor. I asked to see the documented counseling sessions he had had with her. Guess what? There were none. I made him go back and rewrite the annual performance report. He was not happy, but because he had not properly documented the substandard performance, the report would never stick. The next thing I did was have a meeting with *all* the officers to remind them of the importance of continuous feedback, both verbal as well as properly documented good and bad points. You can't set up a team for success without continual, documented performance feedback.

> "You can't set up a team for success without continual, documented performance feedback."

PUT PEOPLE IN A POSITION WHERE THEY CAN WIN

Shortly after taking command of the squadron, I had the second most senior Major check-in for duty. By all rights, he should have been the Operations Officer—he had the seniority and a lot of flight time. However, most of that flight time was not in the helicopter the squadron flew. Rather, he built his hours as a fixed-wing flight instructor in Pensacola, Florida. In other words, he did not have the technical expertise to be the Operations Officer and to lead a tactical squadron.

Nevertheless, he pushed hard for the Operations Officer assignment. I refused to give in. Had I assigned him to that position, I would not have been setting him or the squadron up for success. Instead, I explained the reasons I was not going to make him the Operations Officer and asked him to become the Logistics Officer. This extremely important job can make or break a squadron. He turned out to be an absolute master at small unit leadership and skillfully oversaw the loading and unloading of three Navy ships in several US and foreign ports. During the deployment, I put him in charge of a four-plane detachment, leading sixty Marines on a ship doing independent operations—what an opportunity to grow as a leader! *Setting a team up for success means putting the right people in the right jobs.*

Back to "Sife the Knife." When I told him I wasn't going to war, he instantly recognized *leadership had failed to set up our squadron for success*. Being a competent leader, a week later, the situation was corrected, and we were on our way to becoming combat-capable copilots. He was a man who listened to men under him and made sure they were set up to succeed.

CHAPTER TAKEAWAYS:

Five questions to ask to assure your team is set up for success:

1. What have you done to ensure your direct reports or team are capable of doing what you are asking of them?

2. What education is necessary to do the job? Does your team have enough education, and is the education right for the job?
3. What has been done to ensure they have been given the tools and training to do the job?
4. What have you done to ensure roles and responsibilities have been explained in such a way that they are easily understood? Does your team understand their roles and responsibilities?
5. How are your company policies and procedures delineated? Are they easy to understand?

Not asking these five questions can kill any chance a team has for success. Asking and answering them honestly will set you and your team up to win. It's what true leadership is about.

★ CHAPTER FIVE ★

COMMON SENSE OR LACK THEREOF

"Common sense is something that everyone needs, few have, and none think they lack."

– BENJAMIN FRANKLIN

As I stated in the opening chapter of this book, I'm from Missouri, the "Show-Me" state. I subscribe to the saying, "Seeing is believing," but at the same time, I still support challenging assumptions or ideas that just do not make sense. In other words, use some common sense.

DRUM ROLL . . . DEFINITION PLEASE

I figure it only makes sense to go to the dictionary, for starters. The definition of common sense from *dictionary.com*: "*noun*, sound practical judgment that is independent of specialized knowledge, training, or the like; normal native intelligence."

I wanted to get a second opinion, so I went to a trusted source, *Alexa*. According to Alexa, common sense is a *noun*, and defined as: "good sense and sound judgment in practical matters."

I do not know about you, but I am amazed at how many people are walking around on this earth with little to no common sense. Think about how many people you know who lack common sense. Many are brilliant. Others are not. This situation has been made even worse by technology; smartphones have made these people anything but. Those little screens have further decreased situational awareness, which significantly reduces their ability to apply common sense to decision making.

WANT TO ENSURE SUCCESS?

One of the best ways that I have found to eliminate confusion and ensure success is the "KISS principle." My guess is most of you have heard this term used before. KISS (keep it simple, stupid) means just that. This concept falls in line with the term "use common sense." If you keep things simple, they will be easier to understand and easier to execute.

I've watched countless smart people over-think and over-complicate plans. Then they get frustrated when things do not go well. If they are good leaders, which many are not, they understand they are to blame for the debacle. More often than not, they want to blame someone else for the failure.

REMEMBER, THE GOAL IS TO DEVELOP A PLAN THAT CAN BE EASILY UNDERSTOOD AND ACTED UPON

A simple plan well executed is always better than a complex plan that fails. A simple plan takes far less time to plan and is easier to understand and execute. As you begin to receive feedback and analyze the results, it is easier to modify a simple plan—there are fewer moving parts. That said, a leader must have a thorough understanding of which lines of effort and lines of business will be affected before taking steps to modify the original plan.

> "A simple plan well executed is always better than a complex plan that fails."

NO ONE CAN BE THAT STUPID! WANT TO BET?

One of the best stories I have to share regarding common sense took place in the middle of a six-month deployment to the Mediterranean. This is one of those, "You've got to be kidding me," stories. "No one can be that stupid."

It's August 1994, and I'm on deployment aboard a U.S. Navy ship. This deployment is the exact opposite of the one that I had lived through two years earlier. On that deployment, we hit one liberty port and spent four and a half months in the Adriatic Sea on standby in case we had to rescue a pilot going into and out of Sarajevo. We actually had to do that on one occasion, but that is a completely different story, but I digress.

This deployment was different. We set sail from North Carolina and stopped in Rota, Spain, to pick up gear that was being cross-decked (turned over) from the unit we were relieving. We then fell into a pattern of sailing to a country, conducting an exercise, going to a liberty port, having a whole lot of fun, and then starting the pattern over again. I've never had another deployment like this one, before or since.

YOU ARE SERIOUSLY GOING TO ALLOW US TO TAKE A VACATION IN THE MIDDLE OF A DEPLOYMENT?

At the time, I had a wonderful commanding officer, and we had enough depth in the squadron that a buddy and I were able to take ten days of leave in the middle of an exercise with the Spanish. Our wives met us in Alicante, Spain, and we spent ten glorious days in Porto Colom on the island of Mallorca. We rented a villa for twenty-five U.S. dollars a night per couple. When we walked into the villa, we thought we were in the lobby. The rental agent laughed and told us the whole place was ours. We thought we had died and gone to Heaven! All four of us will tell you it was the best vacation any of us have ever been on.

As you can imagine, the time flew by. Before we knew it, it was time to say goodbye to our wives and head back to the ship. We timed our return to coincide with the end of the exercise. We dropped our wives off at the airport, rented a car, and started the two-and-a-half-hour drive south to Almeria, Spain, to meet up with the ship. We arrived safely, dropped the rental car off, and headed back in time to eat lunch. We were sitting in the wardroom (the officer's dining room) when the squadron officer of the day, Major Bill Smith (name changed to protect the guilty and to make my old squadron mates work a little harder to figure out who I am talking about—my guess is it will take them about two seconds to put the pieces together) came running in completely drenched in sweat and panicking. He was absolutely frantic and wanted to know if any of us had seen the commanding officer.

We asked him what was up. Here's what he told us: The commanding officer and executive officer (second in command) had come out of the field to get cleaned up and head back to a post-exercise celebration. There was only one problem, their rental car was low on gas. Someone needed to refuel the car. That's where Major B . . . Bill (almost slipped there) came into the picture. He was on duty, and things were slow, so the commanding officer asked him to go into town and fill the rental car up with petrol.

YOU DID WHAT?

Major Bill headed out to the nearest gas station and pulled up to the pump. This is when the story starts to go south. Bill removed the gas cap and attempted to stick the nozzle into the hole. There was only one problem, the pump nozzle was bigger than the hole leading to the gas tank. Bill thought about the situation for a moment and came up with a solution that would make zero sense to everyone else but him. Bill stuck his left index finger in the hole and, using his right hand, squeezed the gas pump handle and ran the fuel down his finger into the hole leading to the gas tank. Once the tank was full, Bill put the gas pump handle back in its cradle and paid for the gas. Major Bill jumped in the car, started the engine, then drove away from the gas station. He did not even make it out of the parking lot before the motor died. He had filled a car that runs on gasoline with diesel fuel and destroyed the engine.

When the car died and would not start again, Major Bill began to fret. He had no way of contacting the ship, so he decided to start running. He ran all the way around the port to get to where our ship was docked. Fortunately for him, this was one of the smaller ports that we had visited. Still, it was midday, the sun was shining, and it was quite warm out, which explains why he looked the way he did when he arrived in the wardroom.

Pissed off is an understatement. When the Commanding Officer heard what Major Bill had done, he was livid. This particular commander, "Gator," was laid back, and it took a lot to ruffle his feathers, but Major Bill had succeeded.

WHERE THERE'S A WILL, THERE'S A WAY!

Marines are known for their can-do attitude, and you'll frequently hear them say, "Where there's a will, there's a way," but this was taking it too far. Major Bill was laser-focused on accomplishing the mission. Common sense should have told him the pump handle he was holding did not go with the car he was driving. Despite not knowing Spanish, if he had tried using hand gestures, Bill probably could have easily gotten an answer to his question.

Have you ever seen the movie *Top Gun*, starring Tom Cruise, Kelly McGillis, Val Kilmer, Anthony Edwards, and Tom Skerritt? If so, you should have gained an appreciation for life in the ready room. It can be a tough place. If you have a weakness or do something stupid, you are going to be razzed by your peers, which is exactly what happened in this case. Major Bill's callsign changed in the blink of an eye. I cannot even recall his original callsign, but his new callsign, "Diesel Bill," immediately stuck and remained with him until the day he retired from the Marine Corps.

THERE'S MORE TO DECISION MAKING THAN JUST COMMON SENSE

Two other aspects of information processing tie into and contribute to decision making: situational awareness and critical thinking skills.

An argument can be made that situational awareness is critical in aviation and goes a long way towards keeping you alive. Some level of situational awareness can be taught. As a pilot's experience level improves, they tend to focus more on what is going on around them, which adds to their level of comfort and situational awareness.

The following example will help people understand how to recognize their surroundings and apply what they were experiencing. The example goes like this: You are driving your car down the road, and you see a car a few cars ahead of you with their brake lights on. What do you do? Keep driving along, fat, dumb, and happy until the car in front of you applies their brakes and you end up slamming on your brakes, or do you take your foot off the gas in anticipation of having to brake? Those of us paying attention take our foot off the gas and may go as far as covering the brake with our foot in anticipation of having to brake.

Today, there are so many people walking around staring at their smartphones with no idea what's going on around them. Depending on your surroundings, this can be disastrous. How many times have you heard about a pedestrian who was looking at their smartphone instead of paying attention to what was going on around them who stepped into oncoming traffic and got hit?

In business, situational awareness is important if you are going to

> "In business, situational awareness is important if you are going to maintain a competitive advantage."

maintain a competitive advantage. It is important to ask yourself, "What's going on around me? What are my competitors doing? Is our operating environment different today than it was a month ago? A year ago?" Do you see any market trends that you need to react to?

Critical thinking skills involve using your brain to process the information on a particular subject. It is the analysis of information or facts to form a judgment. Meaning you take in information, use your brain to analyze that information, and form your own opinion. As you are working through that process, if something does not make sense, you have to ask yourself whether the data input is flawed. Is your logic askew?

Leaders with formidable critical thinking skills make better decisions. They are better able to analyze data, recognize patterns, forecast outcomes, and adjust to changing information feeds.

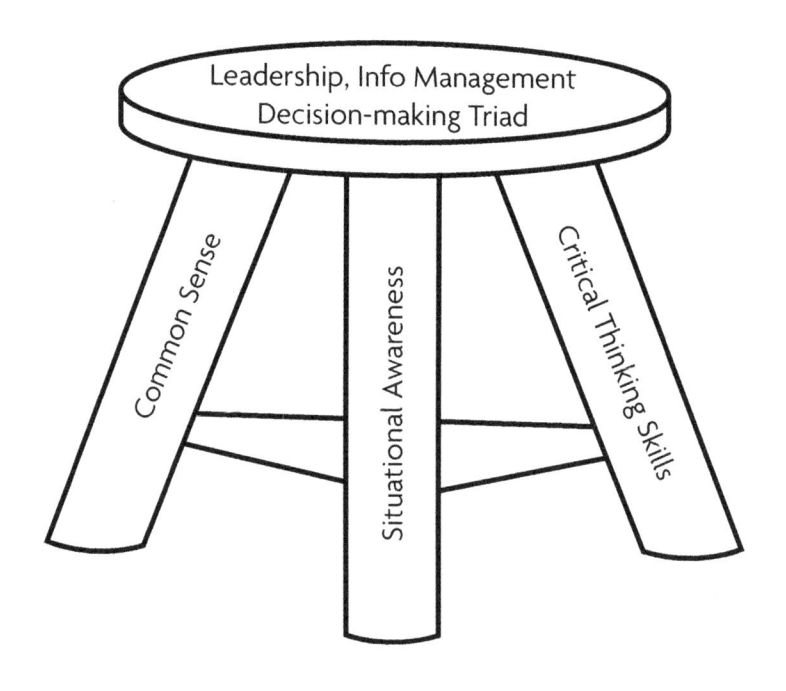

Leadership, Info Management Decision-making Triad — Common Sense, Situational Awareness, Critical Thinking Skills

THE TRIAD OF INTELLECT REQUIRED FOR LEADERSHIP, INFORMATION MANAGEMENT, AND DECISION MAKING

In this chapter, I introduced three important concepts essential for strong leadership, information/data processing, and effective decision making. All three fit nicely together and form the legs of the stool supporting the Leadership, Information Management, Decision-making Triad. Beginning with common sense. A little **common sense** will keep you out of trouble and result in better team performance. When you stray away from common sense, people start to question your leadership ability because what you are asking them to do does not make sense to them. And they wonder if you really know what you are doing. **Situational awareness** helps you understand what is going on around you and in your market space. **Critical thinking skills** are essential if you are going to make intelligent and timely decisions. Applying all three concepts should result in confident decision making.

CHAPTER TAKEAWAYS:

1. Do not overcomplicate things. Keep your plans simple so they can be easily understood and carried out.
2. Ask yourself: How can you make common sense an essential element in problem-solving and decision making?
3. Recognize common sense is never a given. There is a reason they give out "Darwin Awards."
4. Situational awareness is essential if you are going to detect subtle changes in the world in which you live and work.
5. Strong critical thinking skills will differentiate you from average leaders and improve the performance of your team.

CHAPTER SIX

LAW OF LIMITED RESOURCES – HOW TO MAKE THE MOST WITH THE RESOURCES AT HAND

> *"Surround yourself with people who have dreams, desire, and ambition: they'll help you push for and realize your own."*
>
> – KUSHANDWIZDOM.TUMBLR

I previously provided my four leadership points. Number three was the desire to figure out ways to "work smarter, not harder." That axiom came about because I grew tired of having people (who had a lot of time in uniform) tell me, "This is the way we've always done it." They were stuck in time and lacked imagination.

I have flat feet and required a waiver to join the Marine Corps. Apparently, if you have flat feet, they don't want you serving in certain Military Occupational Specialties (MOS) (i.e., jobs), which might not have been such a bad thing. Because of my flat feet and having to wait for the waiver to come back, I missed out on a two-year enlistment that had been in effect for a number of years but was winding down at the tail end of the Vietnam War. Instead, I impulsively committed to four years and shipped to boot camp on an open contract—which meant the Marine Corps would decide where I would best fit.

I completed boot camp in San Diego, California, and then transferred thirty miles north to Camp Pendleton so I could learn how to be a correspondence clerk (clerk/typist). In high school, I took two semesters of typing, so I already knew my way around the keyboard, which was a huge help. That meant I could focus on improving my speed and learning the intricacies of formatting military paperwork.

REMINGTON RAIDER (NICKNAME FOR MARINE CORRESPONDENCE CLERK) IN THE ATTACK!

I initially trained and used an electric typewriter. At the time, fixing typing errors required a piece of correction tape, a small piece of paper with a white chalky surface that you would insert between the type ball element and the typing paper. You would then backspace to the error's location and hit the key that had been erroneously struck, and the chalky substance would go over the black ink, masking the mistake. You would then backspace again and type the correct letter. Often, you would have to backspace and hit the correct letter multiple times to get it to match the rest of the document.

I had been using this archaic method for over a year when I walked in to work one day to find a new typewriter at my desk: an IBM Selectric II Correcting Typewriter . . . the latest and greatest typewriter on the market. With the touch of your right-hand pinky, the typewriter would automatically back up and remove the offending letter. You could then type the letter you needed; this was much more efficient than the previous model.

Faster forward to today, if I followed the "this is the way we've always done it" line of thinking, I would still be using a typewriter, just like I did when I first joined the Marine Corps, as opposed to a computer that allows me to be much more efficient. The typewriter served its purpose until personal computers came along.

When my four-year enlistment was up, I left active duty and went back to St. Louis to attend college. It was 1979, and computers were not yet in wide use. It was not until I was heading out the door in 1992, for a six-month shipboard deployment, that I was introduced to personal computers. Thank goodness I had a young Marine who knew a little something about computers. I used to have to call down to troop berthing and have him come up to my stateroom to walk me through how to open and save documents.

WHAT WORKED IN THE PAST ISN'T GOING TO WORK IN THE FUTURE

Very little gets me worked up. However, if you want to see me get spun up, just say the words, "This is the way we've always done it." Just because we did things a certain way or followed a certain format/process in the past does not mean we should continue down the same path. Everyone—the military, corporate America, non-profits— all face a similar challenge of how to accomplish the mission with reduced manpower and material. I would always challenge my people to figure out ways to be more efficient. The Marine Corps even has a program that rewards Marines who come up with great ideas. My point? Good ideas can come from anywhere.

MISSION CRITICAL LEADERSHIP

"The role of a leader is not to come up with all the great ideas. The role of a leader is to create an environment in which great ideas can happen."

— SIMON SINEK

It is important to set the conditions to make people comfortable and willing to share those ideas. You never know when someone is going to offer up a golden nugget. I once supported a company that did the exact opposite. The leadership team made everyone deathly afraid to share an idea for fear of being publicly humiliated. I do not think they understood they were undermining the company's performance. I spoke to many of the folks in that company and discovered there were some wonderful ideas floating around that would never see the light of day because of the toxic work environment.

> "It is important to set the conditions to make people comfortable and willing to share those ideas. You never know when someone is going to offer up a golden nugget."

The quickest way to get people to buy-in . . . listen and then act on their ideas.

When someone in the organization presents an idea to a member of the leadership team, and it's adopted, you establish instant buy-in from the idea originator. Others in the organization realize you are approachable and are much more willing to openly share their ideas as well. Just be sure you give credit to the person brave enough to share the idea in the first place.

"Working smarter, not harder" applies to small business owners as well. John, my former brother-in-law, God rest his soul, was a fireman for most of his adult working life. Unfortunately, he died from heart disease in his late forties. While he was alive and working as a fireman, he always had a side hustle. In the winter, John was a chimney sweep, and in the summer, he installed landscape curbing.

Firemen know their schedules for the entire year. Rotations are locked in and religiously followed, which makes scheduling side projects easy, or at least you would think.

EVERY BUSINESS OWNER SHOULD STRIVE FOR EFFICIENCY

John was a victim of "work harder, not smarter." When I would go to St. Louis on leave (vacation) from the military and visit my family, I would always spend time with my sister and John. What I quickly discovered was gross scheduling inefficiency. St. Louis is a large city, and during high traffic times, getting from one location to another can take a fair amount of time. John used to schedule a job in south St. Louis in the morning and another in North County or out west in the afternoon. He spent as much time transiting from one location to another as he did on the job site. I repeatedly tried, and failed, to convince John to break the city into districts so he could schedule multiple jobs in one district on the same day, thereby reducing transit time.

This approach would have saved him countless hours on the road, significantly reduced his fuel bill, and allowed him to spend more time with his wife and young son. He refused to listen and insisted on working harder, not smarter.

Let me give you another example of working smarter, not harder: paint rollers. Can you imagine painting large rooms using only a paintbrush? That is exactly what people did prior to the invention of the paint roller in 1940. Using a roller or paint sprayer significantly reduces the amount of time required to cover large surfaces, leaving the brushwork for the corners, baseboards, and crown molding.

Look at the changes in the used or lightly used car market. *CarMax* started the large scale, mass-marketing used-car push. When CarMax came along in 1993, it revolutionized the way used cars were marketed. Today, you can go online and shop for nearly every make and model car. CarMax makes the claim that they are the biggest used car retailer in the United States.

CarMax says it buys any used car regardless of age, condition, make, or mileage, even if you do not buy a used car from CarMax. Appraisals take about thirty minutes, and if you decide to sell, the company will pay you on the spot. Prior to moving to Hawaii a few years ago, I sold two cars to CarMax. They performed as advertised and gave me what I considered to be a fair price for each car.

How about *Caravana?* Who would have thought that we would be buying cars out of a giant vending machine? But that is their business model. In 2018, Carvana was reported to be the fastest-growing used car dealer in the United States. They want you to "ditch the dealership." By eliminating the middleman, they can pass savings on to their customers.

And there are other examples. *Vroom,* a New York-based company around since 2013, allows you to buy a car entirely online and have it delivered to your home. You can explore thousands of vehicles online, find the car that is right for you, choose your financing, appraise your trade-in, and sign for your car. Vroom will then deliver the car right to your door.

And finally, there's *CarLotz.* According to its website, CarLotz was founded over frustration with the process of selling a used car. It helps sellers get what their car is worth without having to sell it themselves and is attractive to buyers because prices are generally below what you would pay at a traditional dealership.[2]

---

2   https://www.carlotz.com/about-us/

CHAPTER TAKEAWAYS:

1. Ensure you foster a working environment where people feel comfortable coming forward with ideas.
2. When you implement one of those ideas, make sure to acknowledge the person that the idea came from. By doing so, you create incredible loyalty.
3. Always strive to find better ways to improve the process, product, or service that your company provides.
4. The goal should be to achieve incremental improvements over time. Whether it be something that provides a small impact, such as an adjustment to a process that reduces or saves time, or a large impact resulting in organizational transformation, constant improvement is required to stay competitive.
5. Be on the lookout for creative solutions that address your challenges and differentiates you from your competitors.

★ CHAPTER SEVEN ★

SAY WHAT? YOU'VE GOT TO BE KIDDING ME!

"No better friend; no worse enemy!"

– MAJOR GENERAL JIM MATTIS, COMMANDING GENERAL,
FIRST MARINE DIVISION, IRAQ 2003

General Mattis masterfully came up with this moto for the First Marine Division on the eve before crossing the line of departure at the beginning of Operation Iraqi Freedom. By using, "No better friend; no worse enemy!" he framed the mindset for the Marines who were about to go into battle. At the same time, he sent a clear message to the Iraqi people. They may not have known the words, but they quickly came to understand their meaning through the actions of the Marines on the ground.

COMMUNICATE WITH A PURPOSE

I've written before about the four tenets that make up my leadership philosophy. Originally, I only had three tenets, but after a particularly bad deployment, I added the importance of effective communication. In this chapter, I'm going to discuss strategic communication as well as effective communication. I see a difference between the two.

Strategic communication is not random messaging. *It is exact communication that aligns with your strategy so that you control the narrative for both exterior audiences and the interior audience of your team.* Strategic communication is communication that inspires and gets people to act in a certain way.

> "Strategic communication is communication that inspires and gets people to act in a certain way."

Let me give you an example from the highest levels of government.

WHOEVER CONTROLS THE NARRATIVE MAINTAINS AN ADVANTAGE

In June of 2004, I was assigned to the Operations Directorate of The Joint Staff in the Pentagon. The Joint Staff works for the Chairman of the Joint Chiefs, who serves as the highest-ranking officer in the United States Armed Forces and is the principal military advisor to the President, the National Security Council, and the Secretary of Defense. In other words, a high-level staff member.

The war in Iraq was a little over a year old, and the United States was struggling to recognize there was a twenty-four-hour news cycle, and I'm not talking about CNN or Fox News. Iraq was on the other side of the world, so when the U.S. was sleeping, Iraqis were wide awake and vice versa. The U.S. government also didn't understand how important controlling the narrative was. Instead, the intelligence community was allowed to drive what information was shared. I will go into more detail on that shortly.

I was the Division Chief for the Information Operations Directorate. One of my duties was to go to the Eisenhower Executive Office Building once a month to discuss strategic communications. During the August 2004 meeting, a proposal was made that involved establishing a White House Communications Command Center that would be manned twenty-four hours a day. The Bush-43 Administration discussed setting up a communications command center that would have information release authority and serve to provide a coordinated U.S. government strategic communication response.

It was designed to be sustainable regardless of which party was in office. The goal was to establish a non-partisan organization that would endure from one administration to the next. Noble goal. Much needed. Never happened. The 2004 election cycle got in the way. Had the command center been established, it would have gone a long way towards countering the terrorist narrative.

A SAD ENDING FOR A WONDERFUL HUMAN

On October 19, 2004, Margaret Hassan, a fifty-nine-year-old Irish-born woman with British, Irish, and Iraqi citizenship, was kidnapped in Baghdad. At the time, she was the head of Iraqi operations for CARE, a major international humanitarian agency delivering emergency relief and long-term international development projects.[3]

---

3   Care International: https://www.care-international.org/

Here was a woman who had devoted most of her adult life to helping others less fortunate than she was. She accepted great personal risk to aid others. Unfortunately, it came at a high cost. Margaret was the first female to be captured in the Iraqi War, and no one knew exactly how to react. They knew what happened to men. They were kidnapped and videotaped making a statement against their government's involvement in Iraq and then beheaded. But that had never happened to a woman. They had never kidnapped and killed a woman.

Did anyone come up with a plan? Did Tony Blair or anyone from his party think about the British response should Margaret be killed? All indications are no.

Sadly, on November 8, 2004, Margaret was reportedly shot with a handgun and died.

There was no reaction from the British or U.S. governments. The only person to speak out that I remember was Margaret Hassan's husband, who asked that her body be returned so she could be given a proper burial. To my knowledge, her body was never recovered.

STRATEGIC COMMUNICATION OPPORTUNITY WAS LOST AT THE MOST INOPPORTUNE TIME

What should have happened? Tony Blair should have immediately held a press conference to address the kidnapping and brutal murder of a woman who had devoted her entire adult life to helping the poor and underprivileged in Iraq. She represented exactly why the coalition forces had liberated the Iraqi people in the first place.

President George W. Bush should have immediately followed suit and condemned this senseless act. Together, they missed an opportunity to speak directly to the Iraqi people about what the terrorists/

insurgents were doing to non-combatants who were trying to help the people who needed it most.

CONTROL THE MESSAGE

One of the more difficult things to watch was the U.S. government's unwillingness to control the messaging. Earlier, I briefly touched on the intelligence community's role in what got reported in the media. In the first few years of Operation Iraqi Freedom, Coalition forces were quite successful in targeting and killing a number of key insurgent leaders. Instead of capitalizing on the impact our forces were having in Iraq, the U.S. government allowed the insurgents to control the narrative.

One of the best examples took place in Western Iraq near the Syrian and Jordan borders. A key leader and several of his men were killed along the border. Instead of publicizing the success the U.S. was having, the government did nothing. In the meantime, the insurgents held a press release stating the U.S. had targeted a wedding party and killed forty-two civilians, including women and children. As you would expect, the U.S. countered with a denial instead of leading with the real story. The U.S. had footage of the attack but did not want to release the footage because the intelligence community did not want to risk revealing a collection source.

Interestingly, I recently read *Fighter Pilot: The Memoirs of Legendary Ace Robin Olds*. In the book, then-Colonel Olds told the story of losing four of his men on a single mission over North Vietnam. Afterward, he discovered the intelligence shop knew the Vietnamese MIG aircraft had changed their tactics to better engage the U.S. Air Force F-4 aircraft but didn't want to tell the Air Force pilots because the secret might get out.

Sad to see that thirty years later, the intelligence community still does not understand how they can contribute to strategic communication on the international stage.

THE BEST DINING FACILITY (DFAC) WITHIN CAMP BASTION LEATHERNECK, AFGHANISTAN

At one point in the Fall of 2012, the dining facility located just 300 yards from my headquarters within Bastion Leatherneck was identified for closure to U.S. forces. The overall commander was concerned about U.S. service members eating under the same roof as foreign national contract workers. We initially addressed this issue by using separate entrances and more elaborate screening for the foreign workers. As insider attacks from Afghan forces grew (keep in mind none of the foreign workers had weapons), this became more of an issue.

If this dining facility closed, we would be forced to use one about a mile away, which would be a major inconvenience for my headquarters unit. Everyone walked to and from work. This other dining facility would have been way out of the way for the troops. Additionally, there was no way for the one dining facility to absorb the hundreds of people from the other dining facility—this was a simple math problem—throughput was the issue.

Everyone knew I had the best dining facility. It was the cleanest and best-run one on the entire base. I refused to allow them to close it. Instead, I started a strategic communication campaign to save my dining facility. I started by telling anyone who would listen how good the Wing's dining facility was. I invited my boss to dinner regularly so he could experience the quality of the food and witness the superior service firsthand. I followed that up with a media event.

SAY WHAT? YOU'VE GOT TO BE KIDDING ME!

I had a large certificate printed up and framed and arranged for a formal presentation to the staff. The presentation took place early one afternoon between meals. The supervisors had everyone gather in one corner of the dining facility. I made a short speech telling the workers, who were all from Pakistan, what a great job they were doing and then presented the certificate declaring the dining facility the finest of all of the dining facilities across the Bastion Leatherneck base. The workers absolutely loved it; they were so proud of themselves. We took plenty of pictures, and I made sure everyone on base was aware of the ceremony's outcome.

Although I had no real authority to make the proclamation, it had the desired effect. The dining facility remained open until I rotated back to the United States. The unit that came in behind us closed it to U.S. forces. That lasted about three months. Consolidating to a single dining facility did not work. The quality of the food went down, and the number of people that needed to be fed each day was just too much for the one site to handle.

My strategic messaging worked. I developed the message, identified my target audience, delivered the message frequently, and achieved a successful outcome.

USE PRECISE WORDS, PRECISELY

When I attended the Marine Corps Command and Staff College as a Major, I was taught to "use precise words, precisely." Words have meaning. The precise choice of words is essential for effective communication.

For example, let's take a look at the meaning of the word "secure" from the military perspective:

- Ask the Army to secure a building, and they will set up a perimeter around it and make sure nobody gets out.
- Ask the Marines to secure a building, and they will charge in, kill everybody inside, and then set up defenses to make sure nobody gets in.
- Ask the Navy to secure a building, and they will turn off all the lights and lock all the doors at 1700 (5 pm).
- Ask the Air Force to secure a building, and they will sign a ten-year lease with an option to buy.

Sorry . . . could not resist poking fun at all the services. Regardless, you have to ensure you use the right words if you are going to get the desired outcome.

WHO STOLE MY CLOCK?

Effective communication means ensuring the message you sent is received and understood so that it can be acted upon.

I have a retired Marine General Officer buddy who bought a house just a few miles from where my wife and I live in Tampa. He also has a small cabin up in the northeast that's been in his family for years. This is where they spend their summers.

> "Effective communication means ensuring the message you sent is received and understood so that it can be acted upon."

My wife was involved in the purchase of their Tampa home. She worked with the realtor and went through a few houses to provide feedback to the couple on properties they might like to see when they began their house hunt. At the time this story takes place, I had never actually been to the home they purchased, but I thought I knew the location.

After closing on the house, our friends got everything settled in Tampa and then took off for an extended stay in their family cabin. A few months later, a hurricane was approaching Tampa, and my buddy called to ask if I could go over and doublecheck the pool/lanai area at their home to make sure everything was secure. I told him I would be more than happy to do that. I jumped in my car and headed over to their subdivision. I pulled into the driveway and noted they had a nice house in a cul-de-sac with a pond out back, just like my wife had described.

I headed around the side of the house, even stopping to say hi to the next-door neighbor, who turned out to be very friendly. When I came around the corner and saw the lanai, it looked like everything was in order with one exception. There was an oversized clock hanging on the wall. So, I grabbed it. As I was leaving, I noted there were a bunch of children's toys in the family room. I was impressed with the amount of unpacking they had accomplished in a noticeably short period of time. I assumed they were all set for their grandkids to visit.

TAMPA DODGED A BULLET, NO THANKS TO MY EFFORTS

Tampa was fortunate. The hurricane traveled up the coast to Naples on the west side of Florida and then shifted towards the northeast, going over Orlando. Orlando received a lot of damage. Tampa remained relatively unscathed; it was mostly a high wind and rain event for us.

Approximately six weeks later, my buddy called to tell me they are on their way back to Tampa. I figured I better return the clock, so I went out to the garage, grabbed the clock, and headed back over to the house.

I approached the neighborhood, entered the gate code, drove through, turned right, went down four houses on the right, pulled in the driveway, and jumped out of the car. I went around the side of the house (this time, I did not see the neighbor). I entered the lanai area and stop dead in my tracks. There, on the wall, was a brand-new clock that looked exactly like the one I was holding in my hands. Boy, was I confused. I put the clock down on a table next to the pool and left quicker than I had arrived.

You guessed it; I had gone to the wrong house. We had a breakdown in communication. I went to where I thought my wife had told me to go. I was supposed to go to the second street on the right, not the first. The houses looked similar, and both were situated on ponds.

When I told my buddy what had happened, we both laughed so hard. Every now and then, he reminds me of the stolen clock incident, and we laugh just as hard as the first time I told the story.

I am damn glad I did not get arrested for stealing a clock. I can only imagine what the homeowners thought when they came home and found their original clock back in their possession. The old one is probably hanging in their garage today.

I cannot overstate how important effective communication is to the success of the operation. If you cannot successfully articulate your plan to the people who must execute it, then your team will not be successful in achieving the organization's goals.

> "I cannot overstate how important effective communication is to the success of the operation."

IN SOCIAL MEDIA, ONE SIZE DOES NOT FIT ALL—280 CHARACTERS OR LESS

One area that can assist/support your business's strategic communications efforts is social media. You must understand one size does not fit all. I worked for a company that loved social media, particularly Twitter, but resisted making improvements to the company website. Twitter worked great for the training center side of the business but was absolutely useless for pursuing government contracts. The website was grossly out of date. Past performance wins were buried so deep that it took five minutes of digging to finally find a disappointingly outdated page that didn't reflect the business the sales team had won over the previous twenty-four months.

Despite multiple requests from the sales team, marketing dug their heels in and refused to make the changes required to accurately reflect the company's accomplishments and product offerings. The lack of support from marketing and the leadership team's unwillingness to look to the future ("It worked in the past; why change anything now?") contributed to the company's demise. Every team member responsible for government contracts has retired or moved on, and that company no longer competes in the government market space.

COMMUNICATE WITH A SENSE OF PURPOSE AND UNDERSTANDING

Strategic communication is just that, messaging with a purpose using words that can be understood.

Effective communication is an essential ingredient if you are to reach your goals. As my buddy Joe says, "You have to communicate, to coordinate, so you can collaborate." *Communication serves to enhance your brand, advertise your product or service offering, and attract business.* Do not allow a lack of effective communication to be your downfall.

CHAPTER TAKEAWAYS:

1. Strategic communications are tailored to various audiences: internal, external, stakeholders, sponsors, etc.
2. It's in your best interest to control the narrative, particularly when it pertains to bad news.
3. The best plan in the world can be derailed by poor communication. The plan must be explained in a manner that ensures everyone understands their role and responsibility.
4. If you want people to get excited about your plan, you cannot be afraid to explain the "why" of what you are asking them to

do. That is how you get them to commit to doing what they are being asked to do.
5. It is important to understand what the different social media outlets can and cannot do for your company (match the right tool to the task).

★ CHAPTER EIGHT ★

DON'T LET THEM TURN THEIR PROBLEM INTO YOUR PROBLEM

> *"If I had 60 minutes to solve a problem, I'd spend 55 minutes defining it, and 5 minutes solving it."*
>
> – ALBERT EINSTEIN

I was taught in the military that if I was going to tell my boss that we had a problem, I'd better have at least one possible solution to offer. Otherwise, I would hear about it.

Regardless of rank, no one got a free pass. There were many reasons for that. For example, there is a saying in the military, *"As you become more senior, your portfolio grows to the point that it is a mile wide and your knowledge base an inch deep."* For good reason. You have a lot of competing priorities that must be ranked from most important to least important. I would argue that if you are doing your job as a leader and letting your people do their jobs, and you are not micromanaging them, you will have a more efficient and effective organization. Plus, your staff will be incentivized/encouraged to come up with ideas on how to do things better.

SO, HOW DO WE FIX THIS?

Too often in the private sector, I would be approached by someone telling me about a particular problem. When I asked them what they thought we should do, they would give me this lost look. They expected me to do all the thinking. I, in turn, wanted them to give me some input on possible solutions. After all, they were the ones who had identified the problem and most likely were affected more by that problem than I was.

> "A team approach to problem-solving usually produces far better outcomes than working individually."

Do not be afraid to share ideas. I have worked for companies where people were deathly afraid of sharing an idea or offering an opinion. When they did, they were shot down in flames or publicly humiliated. The owners of that company could not understand why most of their meetings were a one-way conversation. Often, I think that happened because the owners thought they were the smartest people in the room. Big mistake. A team approach to problem-solving usually produces far better outcomes than working individually. According to William Klepper, Adjutant Professor of Management at Columbia Business School, 97 percent of the time, teams outperformed their most proficient group member.[4]

---

4 Professor William Klepper, Columbia Business School webinar. "Team Leadership: Optimizing Roles and Decision Making (12 minutes, 17 seconds). Team Leadership: Optimizing Roles and Decision Making | Video Library (columbia.edu)

DON'T LET THEM TURN THEIR PROBLEM INTO YOUR PROBLEM

I will spend more time discussing my thoughts on being the smartest person in the room later in this chapter.

> "Leaders who don't listen will eventually be surrounded by people who have nothing to say."
>
> — ANDY STANLEY

I had sidebar conversations with some of the staff and knew from first-hand experience that many people had good ideas that the company would have benefited from—had those ideas been shared and acted upon. People were simply too scared to speak up.

If you oversee an organization, ask yourself if you have created an environment that fosters or rewards sharing good ideas? If the answer is no, consider doing the following:

1. Brown bag lunches where a topic is introduced, and you provide an open forum for discussion:

    A. Start with a light subject.
    B. Ensure you have a facilitator.
    C. Do not let one person dominate the conversation.
    D. Do not be that one person.
    E. If you are a leader, ask questions in a manner that requires an answer that goes beyond "yes" or "no."

2. Conduct a non-attribution survey to identify problem areas in your company. From there, you can tackle each problem one at a time.

3. If your company is experiencing a high turnover, are you conducting exit interviews to see if there is a trend? If not, you need to start immediately.

SOLVE PROBLEMS AT THE LOWEST POSSIBLE LEVEL

My time as a squadron commander (Lieutenant Colonel command) was the highlight of my career. I was finally in a key leadership role, surrounded by high-level performers, in an operational command where the rubber meets the road. It was the best of times and the worst of times. I had an amazing group of people on my team (that was the best of times piece). Then I went aboard a Navy LHD (landing helicopter dock—a large ship that was capable of conducting flight operations with helicopters and certain attack jets and has a well deck). I was matched up with a less-than-stellar Ship Commanding Officer. This Navy Captain, who I mentioned earlier in the book, was one rank senior to me and a bully (a couple of times, he literally felt the need to put his finger in my chest—wrong answer . . . fight's on!). He never did understand that although I was the squadron commander embarked aboard his ship, I still had an overall Marine commander that I reported to.

As difficult as it was for the Marines embarked aboard his ship, it was even worse for the sailors. Before his command tour was over, he had driven every one of his Junior Officers (JOs) out of the Navy. He absolutely killed morale, micro-managed the staff, trusted no one, and insisted on having every problem brought to him for resolution. When I think of the (intentionally unnamed) captain, I'm reminded of something I read on a LinkedIn post from Leadership First, *"A bad manager can take a good staff and destroy it, causing the best employees to flee and the remainder to lose all motivation."* That is exactly what happened.

His approach to leadership was 180 degrees out from the way I operated. My goal was to encourage my team to solve the problem at the lowest possible level. I trusted them, and they knew I had their back.

DON'T LET THEM TURN THEIR PROBLEM INTO YOUR PROBLEM

Needless to say, it was a long thirteen months (six-month workup, followed by a seven-month deployment) with that particular Navy commander. My biggest takeaway from the deployment was *the importance of effective communication.*

I made a couple of more shipboard deployments, and I always made sure to personally meet with the key players on the Navy side so I could introduce my principal staff and walk everyone through my expectations. For us to succeed, we had to perform as a blue/green (Navy/Marine Corps) team. If someone from my team came to me and started off the conversation with, "Sir, there's a problem with the Navy," the first thing I would ask them was, "Have you talked to your Navy counterpart? If not, go away and come back when you've done that." Using that approach, problems were being solved at the appropriate level, and only the most important issues were being pushed up to my level. This allowed me to focus on more pressing matters.

A big part of my desire to solve problems at the lowest possible level was tied to professional development. Over the course of my career, technology changed the decision-making process. For example, an abundance of mobile phones caused problems when the younger Marines had duty. They tended to want to pick up the phone and call a senior officer to help solve the problem . . . hard to grow using that approach. Unless someone was dead, I did not want to hear from them. I expected them to assess the situation, and using their best judgment, make a decision. I could then be back briefed in the morning, and we could review the actions taken the previous night.

SO, YOU THINK YOU ARE THE SMARTEST PERSON IN THE ROOM?

Have you ever worked for someone who thought they were the smartest person in the room? I have. I can just about guarantee that although they thought they were the smartest person present, chances are they were not.

I never considered myself the smartest person in the room. I had good ideas and was probably smarter than many of the people in the room. But I never fooled myself into believing I was the smartest. In fact, I went out of my way to ask others for input on complex subjects or problems.

I always tried to surround myself with smart people and let them do their jobs. I made certain they knew their roles and responsibilities and what was expected of them, and then I got out of their way. I also made sure they knew I would not be doing their jobs for them; I was too busy doing my own job. We each focused on our own jobs and were responsible for our specific areas of expertise. We were all held accountable for our performance, or lack thereof.

As a senior officer, this approach allowed me the luxury of turning the day-to-day operations over to someone else, so I could focus on looking to the future, creating a vision (or strategy) for future operations.

I once had an extremely intelligent squadron mate. From an IQ perspective, he probably was the smartest person in the room. Only one problem, he could not execute. He would come up with great ideas, the commanding officer would tell him to take the lead on the project, and it would never get done. Someone else would have to step in and take over. Eventually, the commander recognized he could count on this individual to come up with good solutions but knew better than to put him in charge of the project.

GIVE THEM THE "WHAT" AND NOT THE "HOW"

Give the team your desired end-state and avoid telling them how to complete the task. There were a limited number of occasions where I would give specific instructions on how I wanted something done. When I did, I made sure I shared the "why" I wanted something done a certain way. It usually involved a recurring problem that I had previously dealt with by learning a lesson the hard way.

THE CIRCLE OF TRUST

In order to be successful, you need people you can trust who can serve as a sounding board and be relied upon to speak truth to power. This is an important concept to understand. Whether you are the Commanding Officer of a military unit, the CEO of a company, or the President of the United States, it is imperative that you have a circle of trust (advisors, if you will) that will help keep you out of trouble.

> "In order to be successful, you need people you can trust who can serve as a sounding board and be relied upon to speak truth to power."

You must ensure you do not end up with a group of "yes" men and women who are going to tell you what you want to hear. It is human nature for the group to attempt to force the "odd man out." In this case, the odd man is the one who tells you what you need to hear, not what you want to hear. The odd man or woman will warn you that you are about to make a mistake. Or they may challenge you with a, "Why would you want to do that?"

CHAPTER TAKEAWAYS:

1. If someone shows up with a problem, they better have a proposed solution to fix that problem.
2. Ask yourself if your organization has an environment that makes people comfortable making suggestions or sharing good ideas.
3. Solve problems at the lowest possible level. Demonstrate you have confidence in your team.
4. Never assume you are the smartest person in the room.
5. Tell them what you want done, not how to do it. Give them a chance to be creative.
6. Make sure your "circle of trust" includes at least one person who will tell you what you need to hear, not what you want to hear. That person will save you from yourself.

★ CHAPTER NINE ★

NEVER UNDERESTIMATE YOUR INSTINCTS AND INTUITIONS

"Trust your instincts. Intuition doesn't lie."

— OPRAH WINFREY

Never underestimate your instincts and intuitions, or mistakes will happen that were easily avoidable.

I can think of many instances where my instincts or intuitions were spot-on, but I was unsuccessful in convincing my boss (leadership) that we needed to go down a different path. None were as costly as the following two examples.

> "Never underestimate your instincts and intuitions, or mistakes will happen that were easily avoidable."

The first instance occurred in the spring of 1996. I was a member of a CH-46 helicopter squadron stationed at Marine Corps Air Station New River, North Carolina, which was right across the river from Camp Lejeune, home of the Second Marine Division. My unit was between deployments and in the process of preparing for the largest amphibious exercise since World War II.

A SIMPLE PLAN, WELL-EXECUTED, WILL CARRY THE DAY

The exercise plan was complex. It involved multiple U.S. infantry units from different services, infantry units from the United Kingdom, and aviation units that had not had the opportunity to train together before the exercise commenced. The exercise would span five states and involve 53,000 troops, 38,000 of which were United States service personnel. Each of the units was at a different level of readiness. One of the larger units consisted of a reinforced infantry battalion (infantry, tanks, artillery, etc.), a reinforced logistics battalion, and a reinforced aviation squadron (consisting of helicopters and attack jets). This particular aviation unit was scheduled to join the exercise after they completed their deployment certification evaluation. Adding additional training requirements to a unit that had just completed a pre-deployment evaluation was not a common practice. For good reason.

Adding to the complexity was the desire, by the Officer in Charge of the Exercise (a Colonel, who desperately wanted to be a general officer), to conduct the main attack under the cover of darkness on a moonless night. This attack would be extremely difficult to execute for even the best-trained units.

TRAIN THE WAY YOU ARE GOING TO FIGHT

Under normal conditions, the Marine Corps used a "crawl, walk, run" approach to conduct training. Training began at the individual level, then progressed to small and then larger formations. As unit proficiency improved, the level of complexity increased to the point that, after several months, the unit would be capable of performing operations at night, with no moon, and, often, in marginal weather.

A normal six-month training cycle would clearly not be possible for this exercise. I was just weeks away from transferring from North Carolina and would not participate in the exercise. Instead, I was charged with training some of the newer co-pilots in the squadron. As a squadron operations officer, I voiced my concern to my commanding officer. He did not see things my way and sided with the Colonel, telling me everything would be okay.

As it turned out, everything would *not* be okay. Two aircraft, a CH-46E (troop transport) and an AH-1W (attack helicopter), collided on that dark, moonless night, killing fourteen people (twelve Marines, one sailor, and one soldier). Amazingly, the two pilots in the CH-46, Major Charles "Chuck" A. Johnson and First Lieutenant Walter W. Kulakowski survived the collision. Major Johnson suffered serious injuries, and First Lieutenant Kulakowski, although banged up badly, walked away with much less severe injures (if I remember correctly, he had a broken arm or wrist).[5]

My opinion never changed. The aviation unit in question, the one that had just completed its deployment certification, should never have been included in the exercise. Their focus was on

---

5   Online. Los Angeles Times, May 12, 1996, *14 Killed in Marine Copter Crash in N.C.; 2 Injured*, by Estes Thompson. (latimes.com)

obtaining deployment certification so they could deploy a few weeks later—Exercise Purple Star 1996 was an afterthought for them.

By the time a unit finished the deployment certification exercise, everyone was exhausted from pushing so hard. At that point, most Marines only have one thing in mind, getting off the ship so they could go on two-weeks of pre-deployment leave and then get underway to begin the long separation from your family. The sooner it started, the sooner you would get home.

> "My opinion never changed. The aviation unit in question, the one that had just completed its deployment certification, should never have been included in the exercise."

That tragic night lives were lost, and families forever changed. On June 19, 2019, a permanent memorial was placed in dedication outside the headquarters of Second Battalion / Eighth Marines (2/8) in remembrance of those who lost their lives on May 10, 1996.[6]

MAKE SOUND AND TIMELY DECISIONS

The second example occurred shortly after I started working for a privately-owned supply distribution company. At the time, we were one of four incumbents on a contract. The existing contract was in its final year of execution, and the client was preparing to release the Request for Proposal (RFP) for the follow-on contract, a contract this small company desperately needed to win.

Just prior to the release of the Request for Proposal, the company decided to undertake a major software upgrade. This was not a

---

[6] Online. Americangrit.com, June 19th, 2019, author Faisal Sipra. (American Grit)

NEVER UNDERESTIMATE YOUR INSTINCTS AND INTUITIONS

simple patch. This was taking down an existing system and replacing it. This was a major muscle movement at a critical time in the company's history.

I pushed back hard, questioning whether the anticipated return on investment would be worth the risk the company was assuming. This was unnecessary risk, that I considered unacceptable, given the company's weak performance to date.

I also shared a story with select members of the leadership team about an event that took place a month prior to the new system implementation. I was representing this company at a fundraiser golf tournament. I arrived early. So early that there was only one other person in the parking lot. I went over and introduced myself to this gentleman and told him who I worked for. He immediately launched into a story about how my company had about done him in 19-years earlier.

HISTORY REPEATS ITSELF

It seems that the company I worked for had decided to introduce a new electronic ordering system in 2000 and did not bother to tell our customers ahead of time, nor did they do operational checks to ensure the systems could talk to each other. The result? This gentleman could not order any supplies for his organization for over a week. The scar runs deep. Nineteen years later, he was still telling the story about how poor planning and even worse execution impacted his ability to get his job done.

But it gets better. At the end of the day, I was in the golf course parking lot with a senior member of our leadership team who did not play golf but joined us afterwards for the silent auction because our company was being recognized for a contribution we made to the event sponsors. Who should walk by? The same gentleman.

When I introduced him to my colleague, he immediately retold the exact same story with the same amount of emotion.

I understood exactly where he was coming from the first time I heard the story. The second retelling reinforced how important communicating with all stakeholders is to the success of a new program. Equally important: the need to conduct a beta test to ensure the new system worked outside of the company's server. We had been conducting a closed-loop test. Why had we not picked a customer to work with to determine what worked, what did not work, and to ascertain how effective our system and training was?

I shared that story with my boss, explaining that we were going down the exact same path. He told me there was "nothing to worry about." The new system was a "pet project" that had been developed and tested internally over a two-year period.

Similar to the rollout in 2000, we were told that we could not notify our customers ahead of time that we were doing this major system overall.

What's the definition of insanity? Doing the same thing over and over again, expecting to get a different outcome. Here we were, nineteen years later, following a similar path. Given the timing, it made zero sense to me to even consider launching this new program.

The first week after the new system went live was a total disaster. The second week was only slightly better. Customers could not order products, and our distribution centers did not know what products needed to be picked . . . complete chaos.

Ten months later, we still had not fully recovered. We continued to improve, but it may very well be too little, too late. There is a good chance this foolish and avoidable decision will cost the company a place on the upcoming contract, or worse, drive them out of business.

The sad part about all this is that, with more of a strategic view (timing, communicating, etc.) this could have turned out very differently.

My point from these two stories: In both cases, my instincts and intuition told me that the situation / environment / scenario was not good. In the case of the helicopter mishap, I attempted, unsuccessfully, to influence my commanding officer to engage up the chain of command to question the usefulness of including a unit that was coming off a taxing deployment certification evaluation. All this just to be able to proudly beat our chest because we were conducting the largest amphibious exercise since World War II. As for the second company, the jury is still out. In its haste to get an inferior, untested, software upgrade on the street the company probably suffered irreparable damage to its reputation.

PATTERN RECOGNITION

I used to see patterns emerge when I would receive intelligence updates and was able to form a course of action without having to wait for an inordinate amount of information to come in. I would suggest that you are probably able to see similar patterns based on your level of experience in your chosen profession. Often times, the company that makes the first move is going to gain a competitive advantage, but bold moves must be weighed against risk. I'll discuss risk in detail shortly.

Let's shift gears for a minute and have a little fun. This exercise is designed to test your instincts. The goal is to put your problem-solving skills to work and see if you can answer the *Brain Game* question below. Good luck.

Look at the five triangles below and determine what number is missing.

```
    2              3              ?
   /\             /\             /\
  /  \           /  \           /  \
 / 22 \         / 54 \         / 68 \
/_____\       /_____\       /_____\
8      3      7      11      8       9

    5              6
   /\             /\
  /  \           /  \
 / 25 \         / 54 \
/_____\       /_____\
4      1      5       4
```

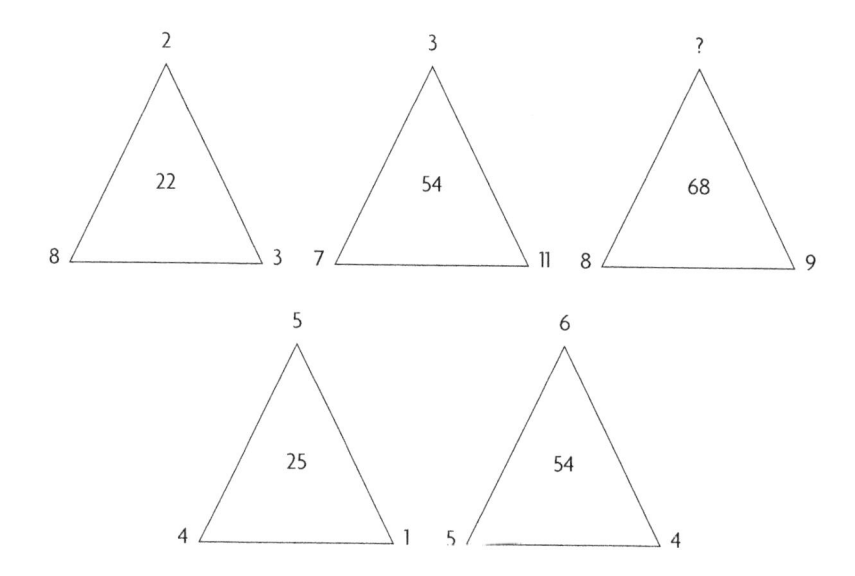

Source: Reader's Digest, February 2020, Brain Games, page 117.

The name of the game: *High Point*, assessed to be of medium difficulty. What's the missing number?

Answer: 4. The number at the center of the triangle is equal to the sum of the numbers at its base multiplied by the number at its apex. For example: (8 + 3) × 2 =22.

If you spent more than fifteen seconds attempting to solve this problem, you were working too hard. In less than fifteen seconds, I looked at the five triangles and quickly discovered a pattern. Once I saw the pattern, I determined the missing number was 4. I then turned to page 122 and confirmed my answer was correct.

This is a good example of why you should trust your instincts. It took me about five seconds to determine the answer was four. A quick glance told me there was a pattern in play.

RISK VS. REWARD

Risk versus reward is a key decision-making ingredient in business. This plays into return on investment (ROI), but it ultimately breaks down to what level of risk tolerance or risk avoidance an organization has.

NEVER UNDERESTIMATE YOUR INSTINCTS AND INTUITIONS

I once worked for an aviation simulation company that had been in business for over twenty-five years. Originally privately owned, this company had been purchased by a large defense contractor approximately a year before I joined. This particular company designed and built some of the finest full-motion simulators on the market and supported two of the best-known aviation companies in the business. The airlines were their main focus.

What leadership failed to recognize was aviation training was evolving. I pushed hard to convince the leadership team to invest in the company's future by earmarking some research and development funds towards virtual reality (VR) simulation. I was unsuccessful in swaying their position despite multiple attempts. They were determined to continue to do what they had done in the past. I was told they might consider putting money into virtual reality simulation in five years; if they waited that long they would never catch up.

The reason for not entering the virtual reality simulation market space was tied to training credits. Presently, the Federal Aviation Administration (FAA) does not award training credits for VR simulation.

What the company failed to appreciate is the fact that the military has eagerly accepted VR simulation for a variety of tasks, including aviation training. The time will come when the FAA will be forced to give credits for VR simulation devices, and the military will have provided the proof of concept. The demand for new commercial pilots will soon outpace available full-motion simulator availability.

This was a case of risk avoidance. The company simply was not willing to invest in its own future. Advance the clock two years, and the company has reorganized three times, no longer has a government business section, and is a shell of the company it once was. All because they refused to look to the future.

The really good companies identify risks and then figure out ways to mitigate those risks. We did it all the time in the military. There were times where missions had to be scrubbed due to unacceptable risks. We took a step back and looked for other ways to accomplish the task at hand.

> "The really good companies identify risks and then figure out ways to mitigate those risks."

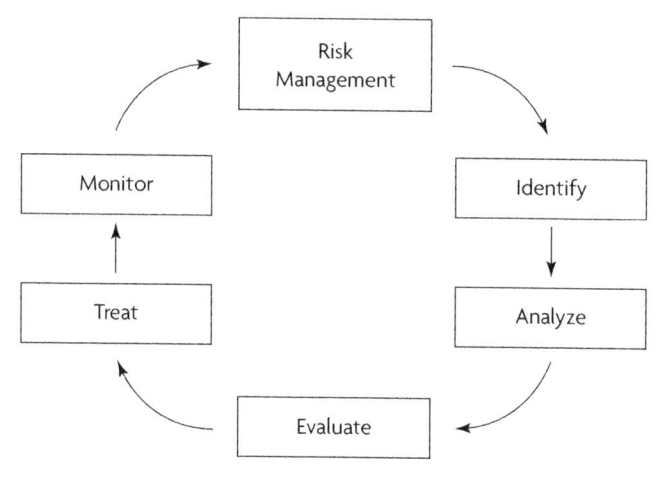

Risk Management Process

There is a variety of ways to deal with risk. The important thing is identifying the risks and then developing a means to deal with the risks, be it through acceptance, reduction, transfer, or avoidance. The chart above is one example. Starting at the top and working our way around the chart clockwise, you can see the risk management process unfold.

Risk identification is the process of identifying and assessing threats to an organization, its operations, and its workforce. For example, risk identification might include assessing IT security threats such as ransomware or malware.

NEVER UNDERESTIMATE YOUR INSTINCTS AND INTUITIONS

In the **risk analysis** step, you determine the probability of a risk event occurring and the potential outcome of each event. In the case of IT, you look at a particular cyber threat and determine the impact a successful attack would have on your company.

Risk evaluation is a process of comparing risks to each other. A weight or number is then assigned based on the likelihood of an event occurring and the consequences associated with that event. The risk with a higher probability of occurring and causing damage would carry a higher weight than one with lesser consequences and a lower likelihood of occurring. Other combinations can be considered, but to avoid causing confusion, I will stop here.

Risk treatment involves developing a strategy to address the risk. Are you going to accept the risk? Reduce the risk through mitigation measures? Transfer the risk to a third party, such as an insurance company? Or avoid the risk by taking a different course of action?

Risk monitoring is a continuous process that adjusts to changes in the operating environment. Risks are never stationary. They need to be tracked, and course corrections must be made until the risk is eliminated or no longer an issue.

> "Companies that develop robust risk management plans are likely to find they are able to minimize the impact of threats when and if they should occur."

Companies that develop robust risk management plans are likely to find they are able to minimize the impact of threats when and if they should occur.

How do you and your company deal with risk? Do you tend to be risk-averse, or are you comfortable accepting some level of risk? With risks comes reward. But at the same time, if you accept too much risk and things do not go well, you are doomed to failure.

CHAPTER TAKEAWAYS:

1. Trust your instincts. If something does not feel right, ask questions.
2. As with instincts, strong intuition will serve you well. Do not be afraid to act on intuition.
3. Look for patterns that you are familiar with to help accelerate your decision cycle.
4. Determine where you sit with respect to risk. Do you tend to be risk-averse? Or are you comfortable taking a measurable risk?
5. Take educated and intelligent risks.
6. Real growth comes from taking risks.

★ CHAPTER TEN ★

WHAT THE HELL WAS THAT?!

> *"A man who does not plan long ahead will find trouble at his door."*
>
> – CONFUCIUS

The aircraft was losing altitude, and there weren't many options available. We were flying over thick jungle vegetation. If I didn't quickly come up with a plan, it would simply be a matter of time before the helicopter I was flying would crash into the ground.

ALWAYS PLAN FOR THE UNEXPECTED

From the first day a student pilot starts flight training, one theme is drilled into your head, particularly when flying a single-engine aircraft: always plan for the unexpected. Where are you going to go if the engine stops working? If you are smart, you carry that thought with you throughout your flying career.

I did and was better for it. I had to put that line of thinking to use one hot, humid morning in the northeast corner of Kenya. I was in squadron command in the middle of a seven-month deployment aboard a U.S. Navy ship. My squadron was one component of a larger unit, a Marine Expeditionary Unit, which consisted of a reinforced infantry battalion, a reinforced helicopter squadron, and a combat logistics battalion.

Combat Logistics Battalion-13 was ashore, working on a series of projects meant to improve the quality of life for the local villagers. Anytime we did an exercise, the combat logistics battalion would work with the local American Embassy to identify projects that would fit in the exercise schedule timeline. If I remember correctly, the big project during this exercise was to complete a wooden bridge that would connect two small villages. The bridge had to be elevated to accommodate the rainy season. The wood used was local and hard as rock; it destroyed normal drill bits in a matter of minutes. Thanks to some creativity, the ship was able to manufacture a drill bit that was strong enough to withstand the test.

At the same time, the reinforced infantry battalion, First Battalion, Fourth Marines, was rotating smaller units ashore to conduct training—patrolling, shooting weapons at ranges, and working on survival skills.

On Sunday morning, February 10, 2002, my squadron was scheduled to fly a long-range helicopter training raid in support of the infantry battalion. Even though it was February, the weather was still hot and humid (the only thing worse would have been working at higher elevations), tough operating conditions for helicopters.

We used six CH-46Es (troop carriers), two CH-53Es (troop carriers), two AH-1Ws (attack helicopters), and one UH-1N (command and control) for the mission. We launched from the ship and flew to a short airfield at Manda Bay, Kenya. We landed, stripped off the heavy chains we used to strap the helicopters to the flight deck aboard the ship, and removed our cruise boxes (collapsible metal storage cases) and life rafts to lighten the load.

Next, we had a face-to-face meeting with the infantry unit we were supporting so they could brief us on their scheme of maneuver. We were limited to using just one large landing zone (LZ). The LZ we used to pick up the raid force would be the same LZ we would eventually drop them off in.

We took off as a large flight of three 46s (sixteen people per aircraft), followed by another three 46s (sixteen people per aircraft), then two 53s (twenty-eight people per aircraft). We were escorted by the two AH-1Ws and the command and control UH-1N in a position where the Air Mission Commander could best perform his duties. We were the number three aircraft in the first flight of 46s. The route kept us a few miles inland from the beach over heavily vegetated terrain.

I was the co-pilot for a newly designated helicopter aircraft commander (HAC). This was an opportunity for the new HAC to log time as the pilot in command of the aircraft—a very important metric in the maturation process. When you are the pilot in command, you are responsible for the safe operation of the aircraft and safeguarding the crew and passengers.

WHAT THE HELL WAS THAT?

"Paco," the aircraft commander, was on the controls. We were approximately five minutes into the flight, flying 200 feet above the ground (probably 100-125 feet above the treetops), when we experienced a huge explosion. We had just passed a large watering hole off the right side of the aircraft, the only suitable landing site within miles.

I quickly brought my scan inside to look at the gauges and saw the ITT (internal turbine temperature—the temperature in the engine's core) for the number one engine rapidly shoot to the top of the gauge. That engine was gone—smoked checked. We immediately started losing altitude. Remember, we were not very high above the trees to begin with.

Paco started to turn towards the watering hole, but I initially blocked the controls. We had a Cobra (AH-1W) just off the right side of our aircraft. The last thing we needed was a mid-air collision between two aircraft. I came up on the radio and declared an emergency and called a "knock it off" for the training raid. I wanted everyone to know we had an issue and to give us plenty of room to maneuver.

Once the Cobra was clear, we started to make a gradual turn to the right and initiated our single-engine procedures, which called for slowing down and dumping fuel. Other than dumping fuel (out of a drainpipe about the size of a standard garden hose—meaning our fuel wasn't draining fast), there was nothing else we could do to lighten our load. We were going down and needed a suitable place to land.

We were too far away from the beach (truthfully, I never even considered going to the beach), but we had just flown past a large watering hole that would probably work. We also had the short runway back at Manda Bay, which was my preferred option. The CH-46 landing gear includes wheels, which allows the helicopter to do a run-on landing much like an airplane does. There's less power required for a running landing, and you can keep your airspeed up. The goal is to make sure "power required" never exceeds "power available." If it does, you will fall out of the sky.

With that in mind, we continued our turn to the right. It quickly became apparent that we would never make it back to the runway, about ten miles north of our current position. Which meant we were going to land either in the trees or at the watering hole.

WHAT THE HELL WAS THAT?!

Ideally, you always want to land into the wind. Unfortunately, landing into the wind that morning would have required an approach to the top of the trees, which were 75-100-feet tall. Then the aircraft would have settled into the treetops. There was too much uncertainty associated with that option. Within seconds, I made the decision to accept a quartering tailwind and land next to the watering hole.

Paco made the turn to final, and as we were approaching seventy-five feet, I took the controls (there was no negotiating, he had signed for the aircraft, but my more than 3,500 flight hours outweighed his 550 or so). On short, short final, I pulled the nose of the aircraft up into the air and almost immediately gave the collective (the power mechanism) a pull up to the point that it could go no further. About that time, we hit the ground. It felt like we bounced, but in retrospect, I think the landing gear functioned the way they were designed by compressing. A half-second later, the nose of the aircraft fell through. When it hit the ground, the nose strut (the forward landing gear) was sheared off.

We skidded to a stop, and the "grunts" (an affectionate term for infantry Marines) ran out the back of the aircraft and set up a security perimeter around the aircraft—just like they were trained to do. We shut the aircraft down. As I was climbing out of the cockpit, one of the grunts came running back up the tail ramp screaming, "Don't go back there, there's a lion!"

I immediately responded with, "Don't worry, I won't!"

That was Sunday morning. Four days later, on Valentine's Day 2002, that aircraft was flown back to the ship. It had sustained minimal damage. The infantry battalion provided security for the site while my squadron removed and replaced the bad engine, dug a hole that allowed the installation of new forward landing gear, and secured a popped chin bubble by drilling holes in the plexiglass and weaving wire through the holes like you would the eyelets on your shoe.

Once the aircraft returned to the ship, it would be weeks before it would fly again. The best news was that everyone, all sixteen people aboard my aircraft (four crewmen and twelve passengers), walked away from that hard landing without any serious injuries.

WHERE IS YOUR UNEXPECTED?

I credit a lot of our success that day with the training I received in flight school that continued to be practiced every time I went flying—always plan for the unexpected. When I took the controls, I picked a point where I intended to land. We never made it there. Instead, we landed closer to the watering hole, which actually worked in our favor. The closer to the watering hole, the softer the ground. When we impacted, the majority of the energy from the gravitational pull was transferred from the aircraft to the ground. If we had made it to where I originally wanted to land, the ground would have been firmer, and the aircraft would have most likely sustained more damage.

PRACTICE MAKES PERFECT... OR AT LEAST GIVES YOU A FIGHTING CHANCE

Granted, there was some luck involved, but *most of the success came from hours and hours of hard work, practice, and rehearsal.* In airplanes, we would pull the power back and practice flying a proven pattern to hit certain points around the farmer's field we were shooting the approach to. At 200 feet, we would add power and climb back up to 2,500 feet and start all over again. In helicopters, we would simulate losing both engines and perform a maneuver called a *practice autorotation*. It allowed you to keep the blades turning as you were falling out of the sky. As you approached the ground, you pulled the nose up hard to slow the rate of descent, paused for a second, then pushed the nose back over. That brought you close to a level flight attitude. You then pulled up on the collective (power lever), which slowed the rotor blades down but allowed you to cushion your landing.

SIMPLICITY CONQUERS ALL

Anticipate the unexpected. In the event something bad happens, you want to work through the issue and come out with that same feeling you had in school after completing a test—"It was easy; I overstudied." Overstudying is not a bad thing. The goal is to turn the difficult into the simple.

> "The goal is to turn the difficult into the simple."

HOW LONG IS YOUR VIEW?

Allow me to offer a couple of examples. From a short-term perspective, let's start with the depth of the bench. Do you have one or more people with specific skill sets that you consider a single point of failure in your organization? If something happens to them, will the company have a difficult time moving forward? If that is the case, you need to quickly take action. You have two choices, train someone already on your staff to perform the critical skills or hire someone who already possesses the necessary skills. It is important to have redundancy. *Your company always must be capable of functioning, including when one of your heavy hitters is not available for whatever reason.*

From a mid-term to long-term perspective, I will give you an example tied to the U.S. government's ability to provide a federal response during public health emergencies. At the start of the 2019 Novel Coronavirus (COVID-19), the value of having a Strategic National Stockpile (SNS) quickly became obvious.

The Health and Human Services Office of the Assistant Secretary for Preparedness and Response is responsible for overseeing the SNS. "The Strategic National Stockpile helps prepare state, local, tribal and territorial responders to react effectively during an emergency when stockpile items are deployed."[7] SNS's main purpose is to provide a managed inventory of pharmaceuticals and medical supplies to ensure the right resources are available and can get to the right place at the right time.

The Strategic National Stockpile's initial response was noteworthy, but it quickly became apparent that the magnitude of COVID-19 would overwhelm the system, which was designed for a regional response.

---

7   SNS Training and Exercises: https://www.phe.gov/about/sns/Pages/training.aspx

WHAT THE HELL WAS THAT?!

Another thing that became apparent with the onslaught of COVID-19 was that the United States, and much of the rest of the world, had unwisely outsourced the majority of medical supply production to China. This is truly a national security issue that I hope the healthcare product manufacturers and our elected officials will correct.

Finally, I want to share an example of a long-term planning effort that we probably all unknowingly benefit from. If you go to the Shell Oil website,[8] you will find a comprehensive description of Shell Scenarios:

> "We have been developing possible visions of the future since the 1970s, helping generations of Shell leaders explore ways forward and make better decisions. Shell Scenarios ask, 'what if?' questions encouraging leaders to consider events that may only be remote possibilities and stretch their thinking. Our scenarios also help governments, academia and business in understanding possibilities and uncertainties ahead."

Shell has some astonishing scenarios designed to improve our lives and make the planet a healthier place. The company is certainly looking for opportunities, but it's also attempting to safeguard against being left behind by its competitors because of a lack of foresight.

Granted, things do not always go according to your plan, but without a plan, you are, as the U.S. Navy says, "Dead in the water."

---

8   Shell Scenarios: https://www.shell.com/energy-and-innovation/the-energy-future/scenarios.html

CHAPTER TAKEAWAYS:

1. Always plan for the unexpected *and* the future.
2. Ask yourself, "Are you prepared to adjust a plan being executed if something unexpected pops up?"
3. Do you understand that by anticipating the unexpected, you will be able to identify issues earlier and respond more quickly?
4. As a leader, are you setting goals that are twelve months out? Three to five years? What about ten years?
5. What changes are you making to set the conditions to achieve your vision?

★ CHAPTER ELEVEN ★

LEADERSHIP IN CHALLENGING TIMES

"Being positive in a negative situation is not naïve. It's leadership."

— RALPH MARSTON

Earlier in this book, I provided background information on the Marine Corps' commander's course. You will recall, this course is where I first had an opportunity to develop my leadership philosophy.

Years later, after I was promoted to Brigadier General, my wife and I would present an hour-long presentation to the incoming commanders and their spouses and discuss how we approached command as a team. I shared my leadership philosophy with them and demonstrated how I had used the four leadership tenets during previous command tours.

One of the other subjects we discussed was what happened when bad things occurred. I made sure the commanders understood these issues were sure to happen while they were in command and that they would be judged by how they dealt with them. This was one of the major discriminators when it came to future promotions and command opportunities. How well did that Marine deal with adversity while previously in command? If the answer is "not well," then their chance of getting another shot at command was slim at best, and future promotions were probably not going to happen.

I had my share of bad things happen throughout my career. In the last chapter, I told you about losing an aircraft engine in Kenya with sixteen people on board. What I did not tell you was the very next day, we had a second aircraft mishap. This time, it was a UH-1 Huey aircraft, the same ones that were flown in Vietnam.

I was in the aircraft control tower aboard the ship when word came that an aircraft had crashed. There were other aircraft flying around the ship, so I ordered one to land so I could get in the aircraft and have them fly me out to the mishap site. When I arrived, I was relieved to see that no one had been killed. The Huey aircraft commander was in tears, and I gave him an extended hug so he could cry on my shoulder. When I let go, I asked him to explain what had happened. He told me he had put the aircraft in a position where the power required to maintain the aircraft in a hundred-foot hover was more than the aircraft engines could produce. When that happens, you have to act fast, or the helicopter will fall out of the sky.

Which is exactly what happened. The aircraft crashed to the ground and snapped in half. One of the crew chiefs was ejected from the aircraft and just missed being decapitated by the helicopter blades. We were lucky no one was seriously injured. Unlike my mishap from the day before, where the engine failed, this was pilot error, plain and simple.

The next day, I received a surprise visit from the Three-Star Marine Pacific Commander. He flew down from Bahrain and then caught a helicopter flight out to the ship. We had a one-on-one session in which he made it clear that if there was one more hiccup, I would be gone. Message sent; message received.

Three weeks later, I was leading a portion of the squadron in combat in Afghanistan in support of the U.S. Army's Tenth Mountain Division. Over the month of March 2002, I redeemed myself.

I deployed to the Middle East four times after 9/11, with the last deployment running from February 2012 to February 2013. I was the commanding general of the Third Marine Aircraft Wing (Forward), which means I had a portion of the wing forward deployed with me. On any given day, I was responsible for 3,500 Americans, 1,000 British soldiers, and approximately 125 aircraft. Over the course of that year, multiple units came and went. Due to unit rotations, I led and influenced over 10,000 people.

During that yearlong tour, I experienced several events that called for strong leadership in what could be characterized as leadership in challenging times. One event that immediately comes to mind involves one of the largest helicopter assaults the Marine Corps had ever carried out in Afghanistan—one of only four Battalion-sized combat lifts since Vietnam.

The mission was originally scheduled to take place on Saturday night, March 24, 2012. Unfortunately, the weather was not cooperating, so we had to delay twenty-four hours. Operation Jaws involved eight V-22 tiltrotor aircraft, four CH-53 heavy-lift aircraft, six AH-1, and four AV-8 Harrier attack jets, along with other coalition aircraft.

The mission involved inserting 560 U.S. Marines and Georgian soldiers into an objective area northeast of our base. The V-22s would be in the lead, followed by the CH-53s. We thought we had things well in hand. And we did, until the first wave of V-22s entered the objective area. Have any of you ever heard, *"No plan ever survives beyond enemy contact?"* This essentially means that once the plan is put into motion, all sorts of variables are introduced.

It was a dark night, chosen specifically so we would have a tactical advantage over the enemy. As the first flight of four V-22s approached the landing area, everything seemed to be fine. Many of the landing zones in southwest Afghanistan were extremely dusty, and this was no exception. The final portion of the landing was done in brownout conditions where the pilots are unable to see the ground. Because of the whirling dust, no one knew the aircraft were landing in a terraced farmer's field. Unbeknownst to the number-three aircraft, they were actually straddling one of the terraces. When the power came off, the right side fell approximately four feet before coming to an abrupt stop. When the aircraft settled, the nose landing gear was sheared off.

Once all the Marines were off the back of the aircraft, the other three V-22s took off, leaving the damaged aircraft in the landing zone. When the first three waves had cleared, it did not take the enemy long to figure out that the V-22 was not going anywhere anytime soon. The enemy started lobbing mortar rounds. Fortunately, the grunts were able to push out quickly to expand the security perimeter, and the mortar rounds stopped before the enemy could find their intended target.

The following morning, the squadron flew a maintenance recovery team and a team of combat engineers from the Marine Wing Support Squadron to the mishap site. It was now a race against the clock—that aircraft had to be out of the field by the time the battalion was extracted on Friday, or we were going to be in trouble. I did not want to have to blow the aircraft in place. If I had done that, chances were the enemy would have still claimed they blew the aircraft up and achieved a moral victory.

It was determined that the squadron could make the repairs necessary to fly the aircraft back to our home airfield at Bastion/Leatherneck. This proved easier said than done. After the site survey, the commanders and their teams worked together to formulate a repair and recovery plan. They provided "in-progress reviews," and when they were ready, a formal plan was presented and approved.

All this was done in a matter of hours. The road march from Bastion/Leatherneck up to the mishap site took thirty hours. The transit time took longer than originally projected because of an extensive improvised explosive device (IED) belt that lay between the point where the convoy left the hard surface road and the aircraft.

The ground repair work was accomplished swiftly, and the aircraft was flown back to the airfield at sunset on Wednesday. I happened to be returning from a mission with a CH-53E squadron and was sitting on the flight line and got to see the V-22 land on a stack of wooden pallets and a mattress. Once the aircraft had safely landed, we were able to claim, "mission accomplished!"

To put things in context, safely recovering the V-22 was probably the best thing that happened all week. On Monday, in Lashkar Gah, an Afghanistan National Army (ANA) soldier opened fire on British troops manning an entry point. Two British soldiers were killed, one wounded, and the ANA soldier was killed. That same day, five Afghanistan National Security Force personnel were killed.

On Tuesday, we had a ramp ceremony (a memorial service held on the flight line) at 8:30 pm for the five Afghanistan National Army soldiers killed and a second ramp ceremony at 11:00 pm for a Marine Logistics Group Marine who died while checking on an IED earlier that day. On Wednesday, the British conducted a vigil (the British version of a memorial service) for three soldiers who had been killed in the past week. One was a Captain just four days away from going home. The other two were the two soldiers killed in Lashkar Gah on Monday. On Thursday, there was a ramp ceremony for a Ninth Engineer Support Battalion Marine who was killed in action. On Friday, there was a ramp ceremony for a Light Attack Reconnaissance Marine killed when his LAV (Light

Armored Vehicle. The vehicle is thin skinned, has eight rubber tires and some firepower. It does not have a tank turret) hit an IED. An hour later, we were back on the ramp for an ANA soldier who had been killed. It was a really tough week, to say the least.

Fortunately, you do not normally have to deal with life or death issues in corporate America. Leaders in the private sector often face challenges on a different level. That said, those challenges still need to be addressed.

Depending on the size of your organization and the market space you occupy, you may have to deal with: integrity/ethics issues; changing operating environments (be it from increased competition, changing regulations, etc.); finding the right people through your recruiting, hiring, and retaining efforts; inspiring the workforce; or problem-solving and risk management.

I have consulted for companies that struggled with integrity and ethics issues as well as witnessed competition using questionable business practices. I do not know how these companies think they will be able to retain customers/clients when they stretch the truth or lie outright. Over the long haul, this approach is unsustainable.

Finding the right people through your recruiting, hiring, and retaining efforts is always a challenge. I will offer a couple of thoughts. First, do you have an internship program in place? There's nothing wrong with putting prospective employees through a dress rehearsal. This allows you to get to know the person better and ensure they have the requisite skills and work ethic that the company is seeking. Second, if you have doubts, particularly in more senior positions, consider bringing the person on in a 1099 status. Have them sign a non-disclosure agreement and a non-compete clause and offer them a six-month to twelve-month contract. That allows both parties to get to know each other better and ensure they are a good fit.

It is easy to lead when things are going well. *True leaders rise to the occasion when challenges present themselves.* Instead of seeing obstacles,

LEADERSHIP IN CHALLENGING TIMES

they see opportunities. Instead of causing panic, they provide a calming presence.

CHAPTER TAKEAWAYS:

1. An effective crisis response requires having the right team to address the problem, develop a suitable solution, and execute the approved plan.
2. Unethical behavior is never acceptable. How does your company deal with integrity/ethical issues? Is it tolerated in the name of profit? Or do they do the right thing and ask themselves, "What do we stand for?"
3. Effective leadership is key to a company's success. But you must have someone to lead. It is important to have the right people on your team. Invest in your company's future by ensuring you have a qualified human resources representative/department and proven recruiting, hiring, and retaining practices in place.
4. Do not be afraid to be creative and turn innovative ideas into reality.

★ CHAPTER TWELVE ★

LEADERS NEVER STOP LEARNING

"Leadership and learning are indispensable to each other."

– JOHN F. KENNEDY

As this chapter title asserts, leaders never stop learning, and as John F. Kennedy so eloquently states, *"Leadership and learning are commingled."* Regardless of your profession, you should never stop learning. For a couple of reasons. First and foremost, there is a reason there are so many books written on leadership and management. Leadership requires constant improvement. Second, no one person has all the answers to being an effective leader. Time drives change, the working environment changes, and information requirements change. To remain relevant, you must continue to seek formal education opportunities and self-educate whenever possible.

LEADERS NEVER STOP LEARNING

One measurable benefit of being on active duty is the educational opportunities afforded to service members throughout their careers. For Marine officers, our training begins at Officer Candidate School and continues at The Basic School. From there, we went on to our military occupation specialty generating school. Later, we would have opportunities to spend a year in resident school as Captains, again as Majors, and as Lieutenant Colonels. Formal education did not end there. When I made Brigadier General, I was required to attend a Professional Military Education course every year. Why all the schooling? We studied different levels of operations and strategy in each course. Resident courses also offered a degree of cross-pollination—from the exposure to Marines with different backgrounds and an introduction to officers from other services, as well as U.S. government officials and officers from allied nations.

As I was preparing to leave active duty, I decided to make myself more valuable to future employers. I took advantage of a program Syracuse University offered: the Veteran's Career Transition Program (VCTP). I used that program to become certified as a Program Management Professional (PMP). Not because I wanted to be a program manager. I wanted to be the boss of program managers and needed to be able to ask intelligent questions. I also did it to demonstrate I was willing to take on a challenge and learn something new.

LEADERSHIP IS EVERYTHING

In this book, I have shared my leadership philosophy with you. I applied the four tenets of that philosophy to every level of command I had as well as used them in the private sector. They have proven to work in multiple settings. By applying my leadership philosophy, you will build a stronger, more resilient, and effective team. Your employees will be happier, more productive, and loyal.

WHEN THEY SUCCEED, YOU SUCCEED, AND EVERYONE WINS!

Your success depends on your peoples' success, so setting them up for success should be your number one goal. By investing in your employee's future, you invest in the future of your company. They may or may not stay with you. If they leave to go to another company, get over it. You will find a suitable replacement, and you never know—you might even find someone even more qualified than the person who left. Remind yourself that leaders can be found at every level of an organization. Ensure those leaders are working with you and not against you. Finally, strong leadership ensures success.

THE LEADERSHIP, INFORMATION MANAGEMENT, AND DECISION-MAKING TRIAD

Many companies are saddled with intelligent leaders who lack common sense. These people tend to overthink or complicate plans unnecessarily when the exact opposite should be taking place. By simplifying your life, plans, and policies, you will become more focused and productive.

Common sense is essential in problem-solving and decision making, but it does not stand alone. Situational awareness is required to detect subtle changes in the environment around you. Couple those two with strong critical thinking skills, and you have a winning recipe. Together, those three ingredients form the leadership, information management, and decision-making triad. Remove one aspect of the triad, and you immediately create an unbalanced situation.

NO COMPANY ENJOYS AN ABUNDANCE OF RESOURCES

Whether you are in the military, part of a publicly-traded company, or a privately owned company, you will never have enough resources, be it manpower, material, or money. For that reason, it is important to figure out how to operate more efficiently. That is one reason Lean Six Sigma was created—to improve performance by systematically removing waste and reducing variation. In other words, Lean Six Sigma streamlines processes, saves time, as well as money.

Think about it, the idea for Lean Six Sigma had to start somewhere. The working conditions had to be such that people were not afraid to share new ideas. Ideally, your organization allows people to be creative in thought and express their ideas without fear of embarrassment. Good ideas can come from anywhere. When acted upon appropriately, they can yield huge dividends in the form of greater savings, increased profits, or improved customer satisfaction. Who wouldn't want that?

It also serves as a motivator for the workforce. When someone comes up with a good idea, and it is implemented, others see their colleague was listened to, resulting in other employees putting on their thinking caps and coming up with their own useful ideas.

EFFECTIVE COMMUNICATION IS ESSENTIAL FOR SUCCESSFUL LEADERS

Successful leaders must be able to communicate with a wide variety of stakeholders, employees, the board of directors, shareholders, and the media. The ones who do it well tailor the message for the audience and always control the narrative, particularly bad news. They use oral and written communications to explain the "why" behind their plan, which gets people excited about the project and gains their support. Effective communication skills are one of the most important leadership attributes. So much of your success as a leader resides in your ability to communicate effectively.

> "So much of your success as a leader resides in your ability to communicate effectively."

PROBLEM-SOLVING IS A TEAM SPORT

Excellent leaders can look at challenges, see opportunities, and offer solutions, but they do not have all the answers. Problem-solving should take place at all levels. Do not allow employees to turn their problem into your problem. When an employee approaches you with a problem, they need to also offer a proposed solution. If they do not, turn them around and tell them to come back when they have at least one realistic recommendation for solving the problem. This is a great skill to develop in your workforce—they benefit, and so does the organization. Employees who are problem solvers are highly sought after in every industry. You are encouraged to challenge your human resource departments to find problem solvers as part of the recruiting process.

TRUSTING YOUR INSTINCTS AND INTUITIONS LEADS TO BETTER DECISIONS

How many times have you faced a situation where your instincts or intuitions told you to act, yet you hesitated? What did that cost you? Did you miss out on an opportunity? Or lose money because you allowed a process that your intuition told you was not working as well as it should to continue instead of correcting the situation? Trust your instincts and intuitions and look for patterns you are familiar with to help accelerate your decision cycle.

LISTEN TO YOUR BODY

Between your head, your heart, and your stomach, your body will let you know if you are screwing up. Our bodies have a way of responding to bad decisions. Some people get a stomachache, others lose sleep. If you find yourself feeling out of sorts after making a particularly difficult decision, you may want to go back and revisit that decision.

ALWAYS BE THINKING AND LOOKING AHEAD

Companies are more likely to do well if they conduct both long-range planning and crisis management planning. Long-range planning focuses on a vision and lays out the steps required to achieve the desired goal. Crisis management planning identifies areas that might arise and impact the company's operations. By anticipating the unexpected, you will be able to identify issues earlier and respond more quickly, thereby minimizing the damage.

LEADERSHIP IN CHALLENGING TIMES

The world is changing quickly, and we must keep pace with changes, or we will no longer be relevant. This is true at the individual as well as organizational level. This is one reason many professions require annual professional training—they want their practitioners to stay up to date on new techniques and procedures and comply with state and federal regulations. In some cases, such as the medical community, this is done to ensure safety and prevent harm to patients.

THE LAST THREE WORDS ON LEADERSHIP

Finally, the best leadership advice I have to offer is to **lead by example**. You cannot go wrong with that approach.

Hopefully, this book captured your attention, and you found my vignettes both entertaining and educational. My goal was to share concepts and ideas for you to think about—and provide tools and tips that you can apply to help you *act* strategically, *execute* flawlessly, and *lead* effectively. With any luck, I achieved my objectives.

Semper Fidelis,

GREGG A. STURDEVANT
MAJOR GENERAL
UNITED STATES MARINE
CORPS (RETIRED)

★ READY FOR MORE? ★

Are you:

- Challenged by a current crisis?
- Ready to take your organization to the next level?
- Want to grow personally and professionally?

Discover how Gregg Sturdevant and Mission Critical Leadership Solutions can help with a complementary consultation. To schedule your session please send an email to:

gregg@missioncriticalcoaching.net

with a short note indicating what you would like to accomplish on the call.

ACKNOWLEDGEMENT

A special thanks to Howard VanEs and his team at Let's Write Books, Inc. Through Howard's guidance and his team's expertise the manuscript for this book went from an unpolished product to a professionally edited and designed book.

ABOUT THE AUTHOR

M ajor General Gregg A. Sturdevant served in the Marine Corps from July 1975 to January 2015. As a Naval Aviator, he amassed 4,500 hours, primarily in the CH-46E helicopter.

Over the course of his career, Major General Sturdevant deployed ten times. The last four of those deployments came after 9/11, and all four were to the Middle East.

His final operational assignment was as the Commanding General, Third Marine Aircraft Wing (Forward) and Commanding General, Bastion/Leatherneck Complex from February 2012 through February 2013 in support of Operation Enduring Freedom 12 in Helmand Province, Afghanistan.

ABOUT THE AUTHOR

He had numerous assignments in the Pentagon and with upper-level staff, covering a wide-ranging portfolio. As a general officer, Gregg served as the Director of Public Affairs for the Marine Corps, led a hundred-person operations/intelligence team in the National Military Command Center, developed and executed a $27 billion-dollar annual budget for the Marine Corps, and served as the Director of Strategic Planning and Policy for the United States Pacific Command.

Gregg brings with him extensive senior executive leadership and strong project management experience in complex organizations undergoing constant change.

Since retiring from active duty, Gregg has served as a business development consultant and worked for a large publicly traded defense contractor and a small privately-owned company.

Gregg founded Mission Critical Leadership Solutions to continue to serve with a focus on individual professional development and improved company performance. He's taken the experience and expertise gained while in uniform and added that to what he's learned over the last few years to come up with a winning solution that, first and foremost, sets clients up for success!

You are invited to check out Gregg's Mission Critical Leadership Solutions website at:

www.missioncriticalcoaching.net

Made in the USA
Las Vegas, NV
05 May 2021